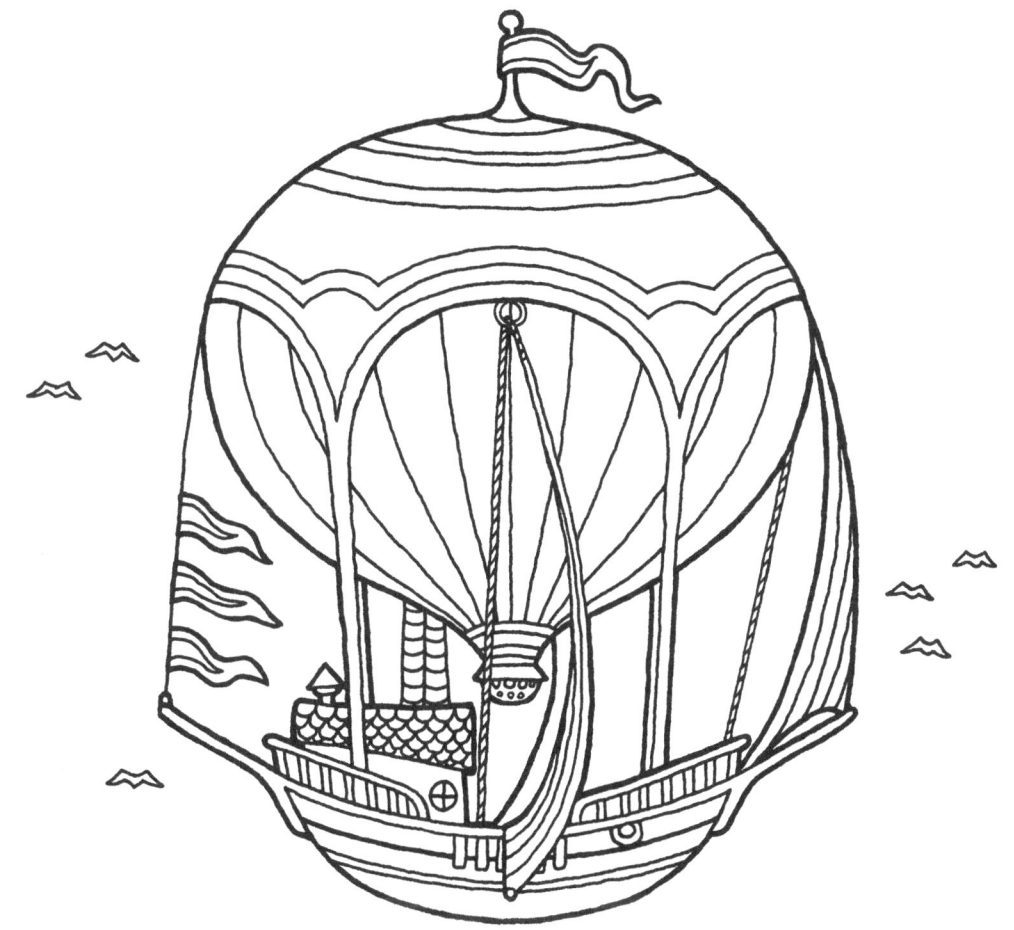

AIRSHIP ADVENTURES

ILLUSTRATED BY
EMILY M. ALLIN

Emily M. Allin
WWW.EMILYALLIN.ART

Airship Adventures started out as two small whimsical doodles which, for the longest time, were hidden in the pages of one of my art books. Out of sight and out of mind I rediscovered them one day and thought "These could be a coloring book." The idea instantly lit up my imagination with possibilities. I was inspired, so I got to work. This idea became a plan that, miraculously, I stuck to over the course of many years. Through painful lulls in motivation, particularly frustrating images, and simply the absence of free time, I somehow found the time. Possibility became reality.

I will take this moment to thank my parents for their Graphic Arts know-how, guidance and efforts in making this book happen, and to thank my sister, Amanda, for agreeing to pose for me on so many occasions. This coloring book is the result of sticking to an idea until the end. I hope it inspires you, in one way or another. ~ Em

Copyright © 2018
by Emily M. Allin

All rights reserved.

No part of this book may be reproduced in whole or in part in any form.

ISBN: 978-1-7326990-1-4

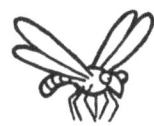
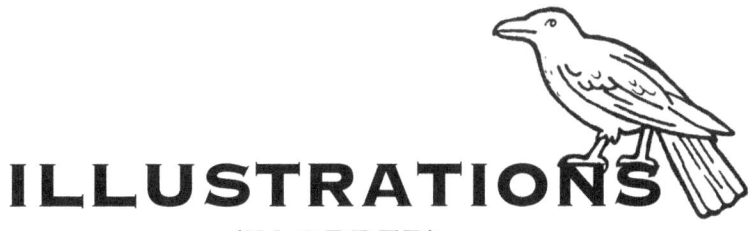

ILLUSTRATIONS
(IN ORDER)

Windy Way
Make the Flight
The Anchor
Patches
Ropey Rig
Sunrise Circle
Sunny Sails
Starry
Flying Fishing
Diamond Vine
Some Flowers
Blast Off
Pulley Punks
Adventures Ahead
Monkey Landing

Fancy Flyers
Blooming Lattice
The Crash
Light the Night
Deco
Fowl Flight
The Thief
High Frontier
Doyle
Nymph Navigation
Oasis
Compass
Ship Shape
Sea and Sky
Weather the Storm

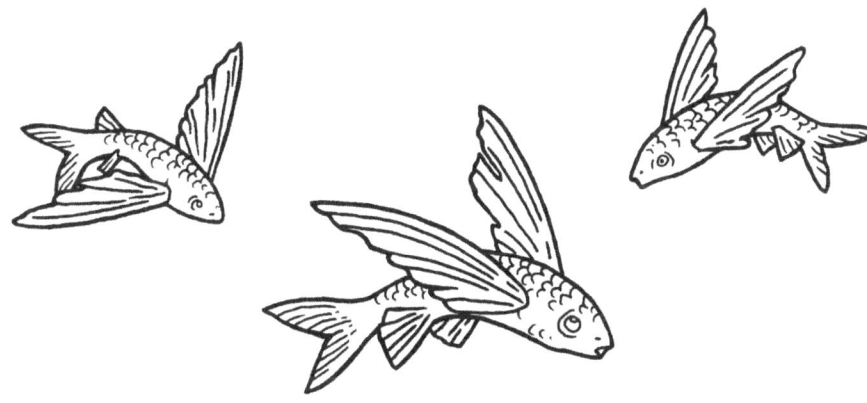

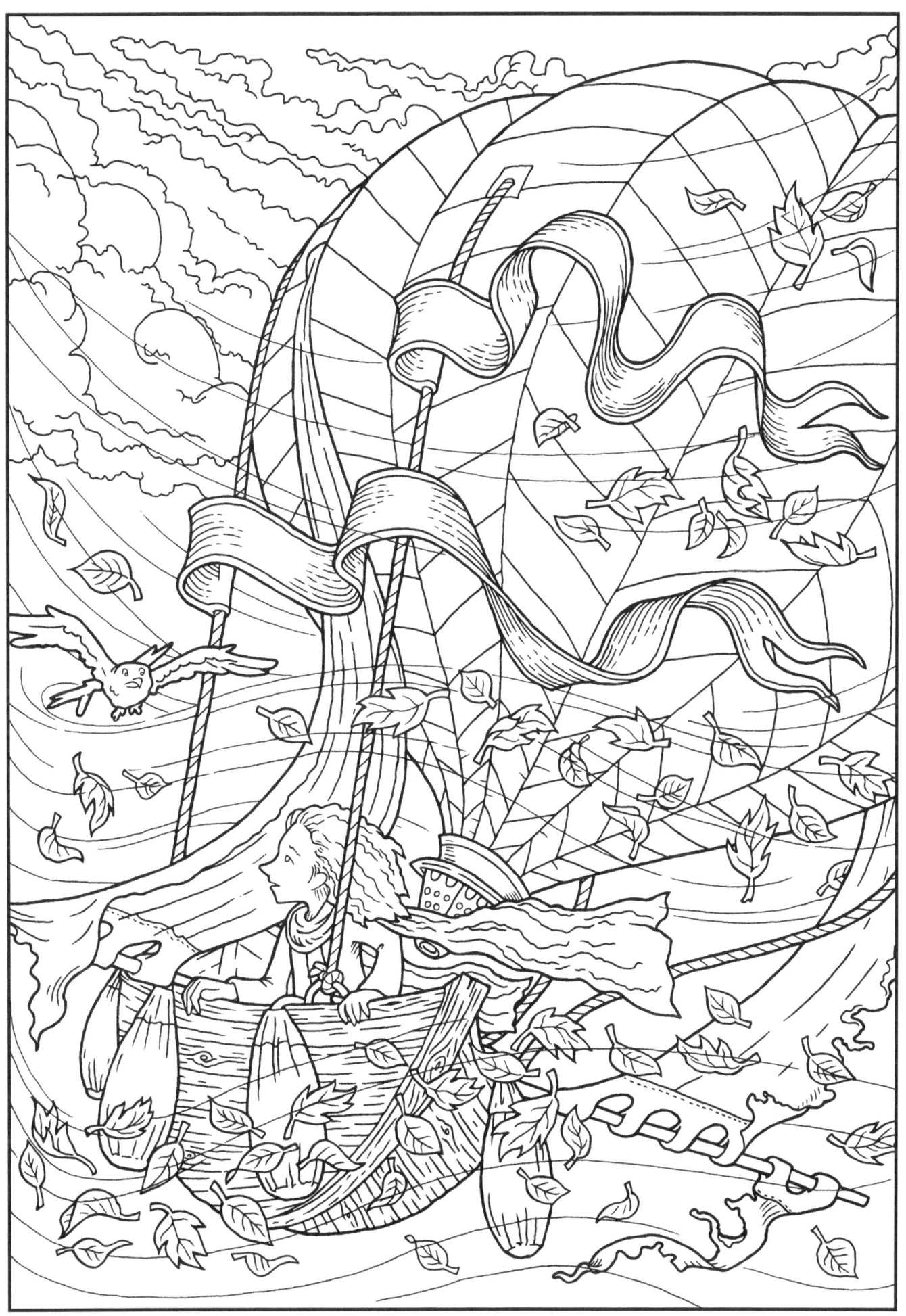

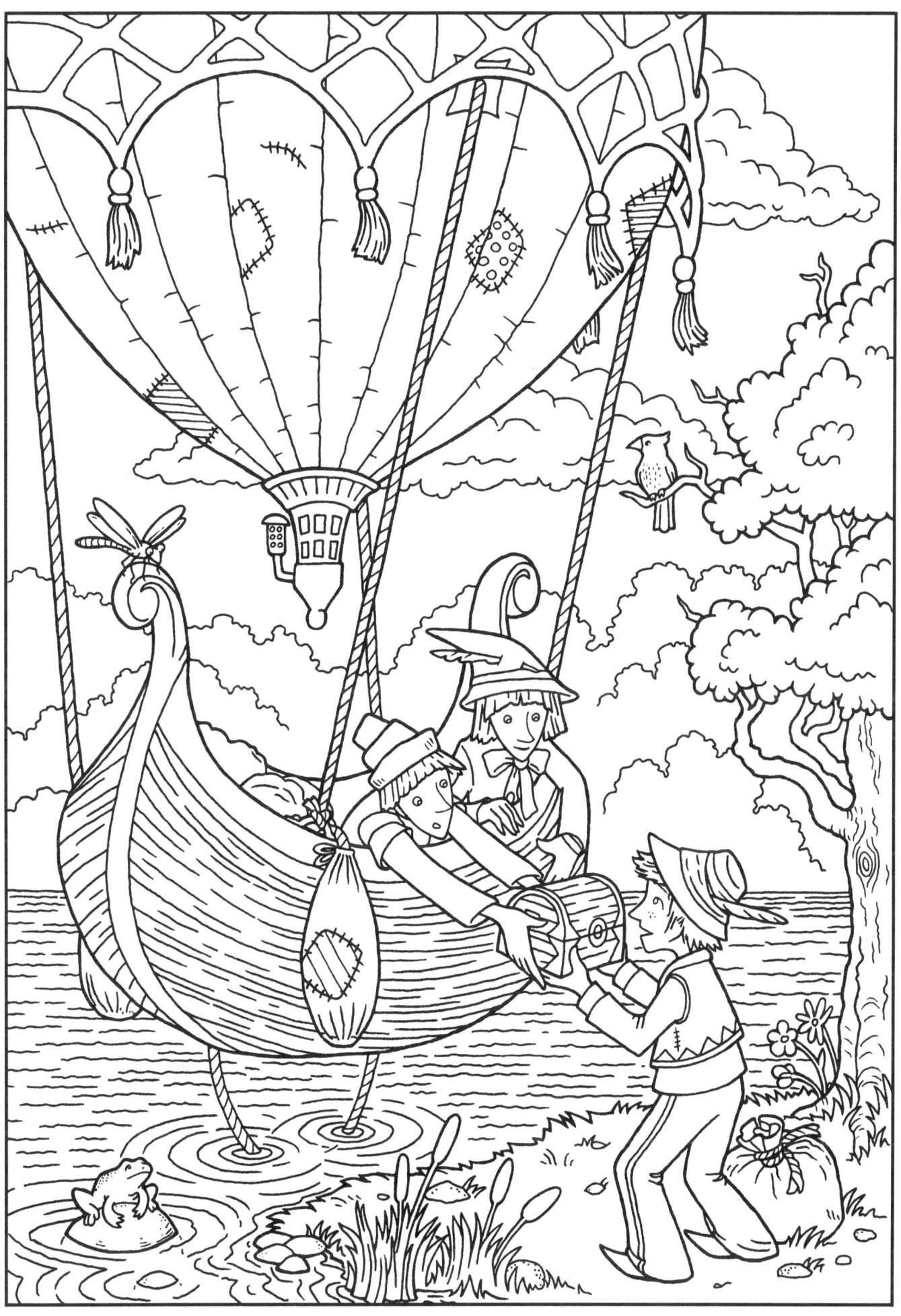

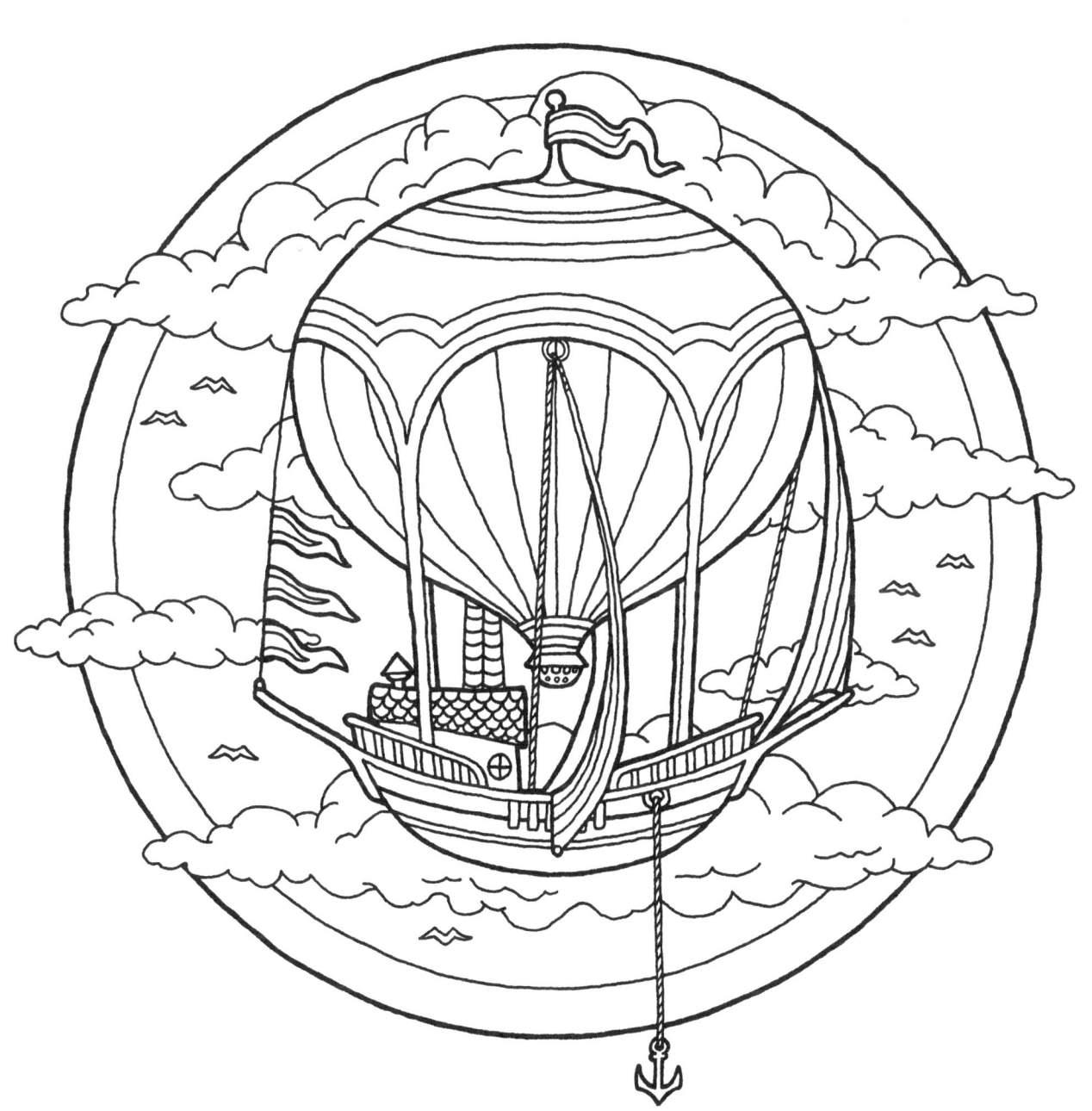

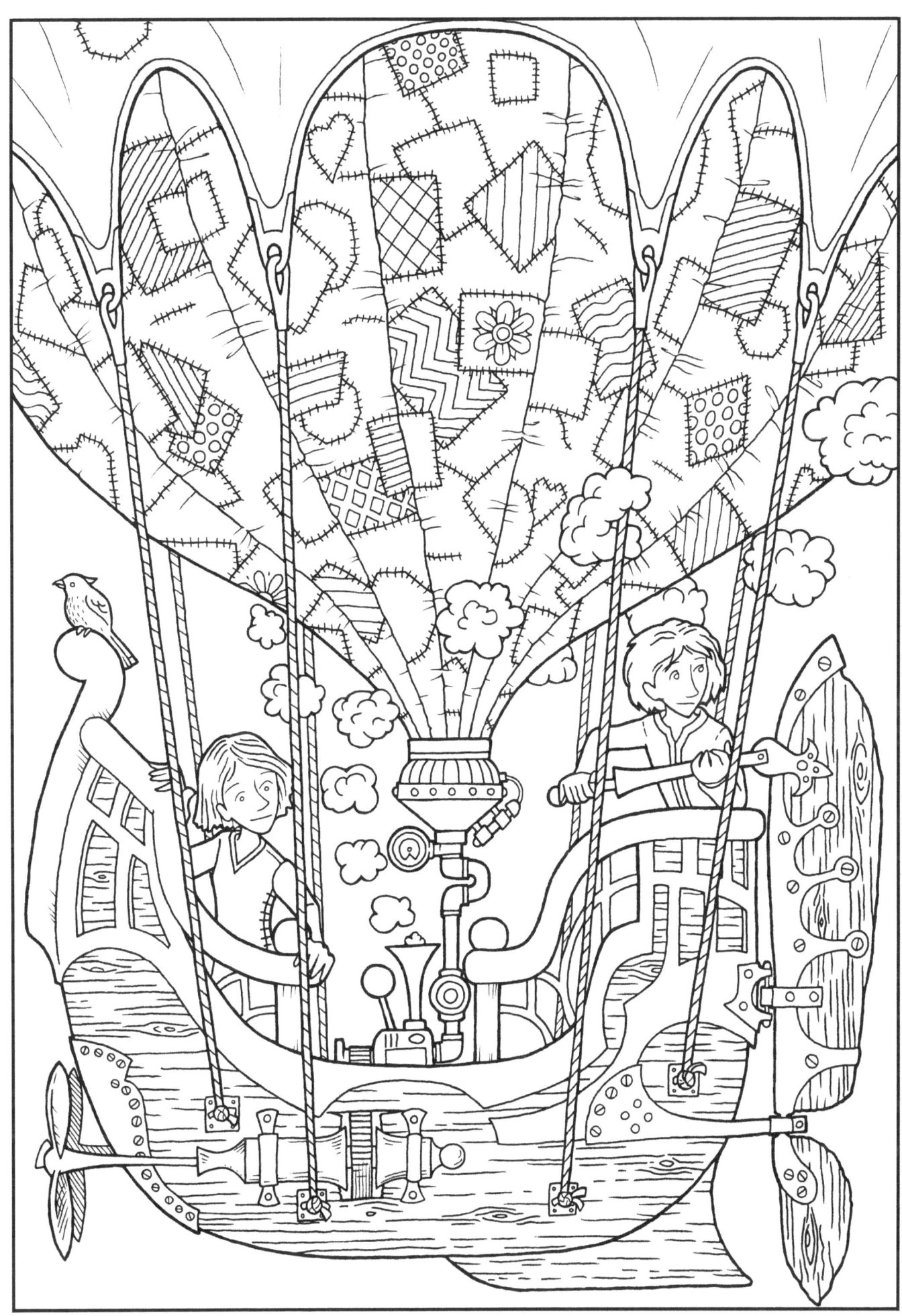

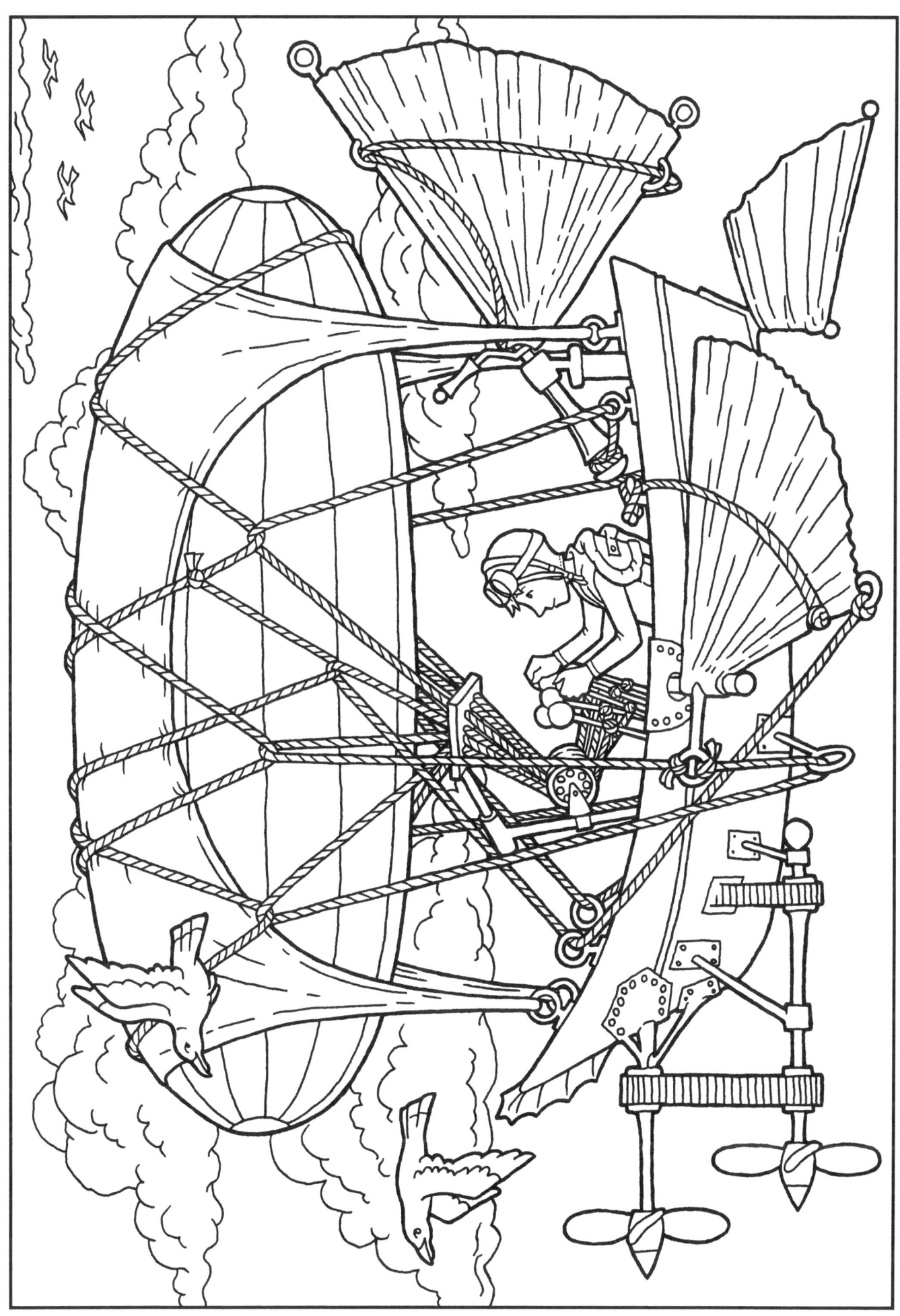

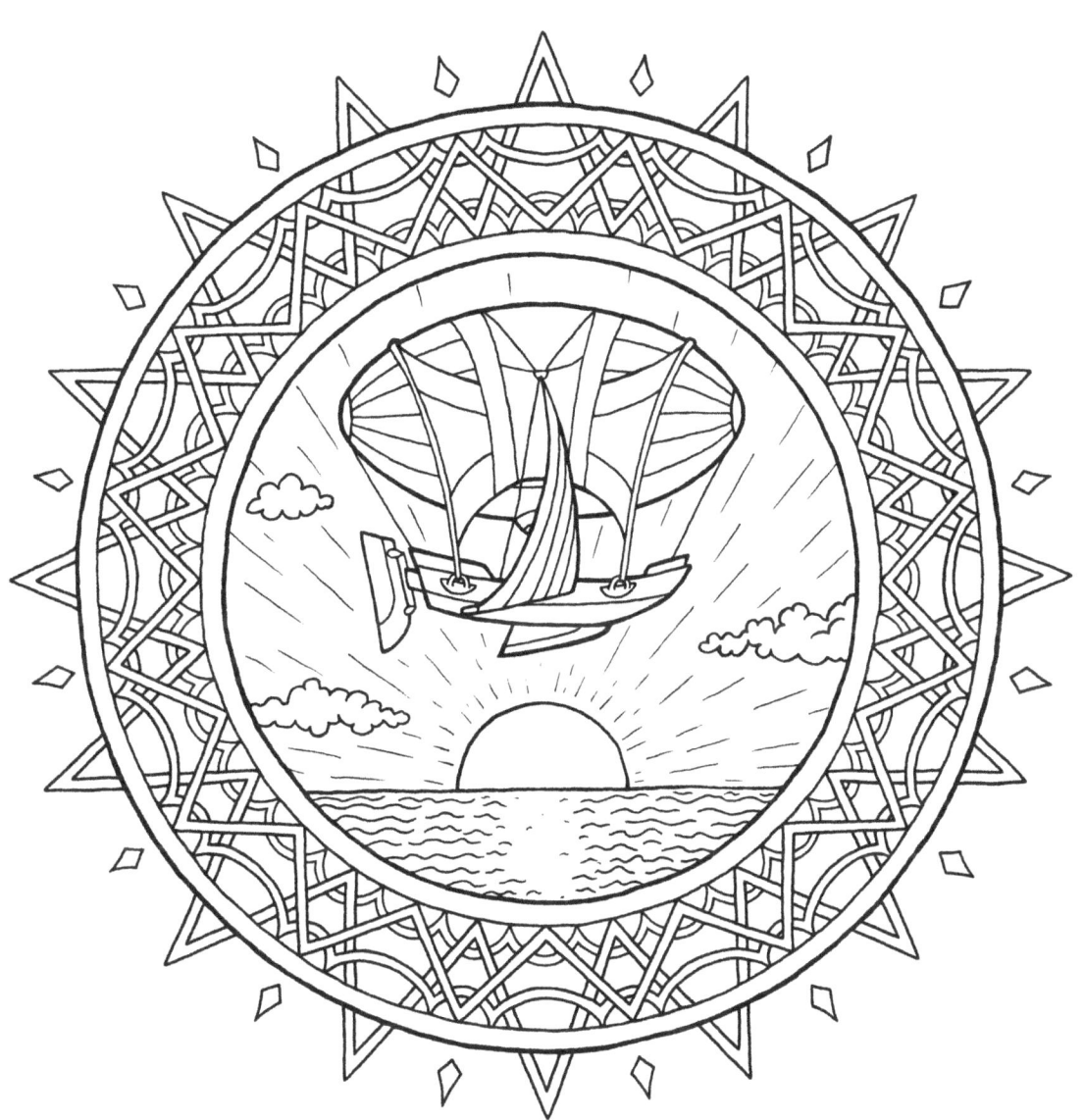

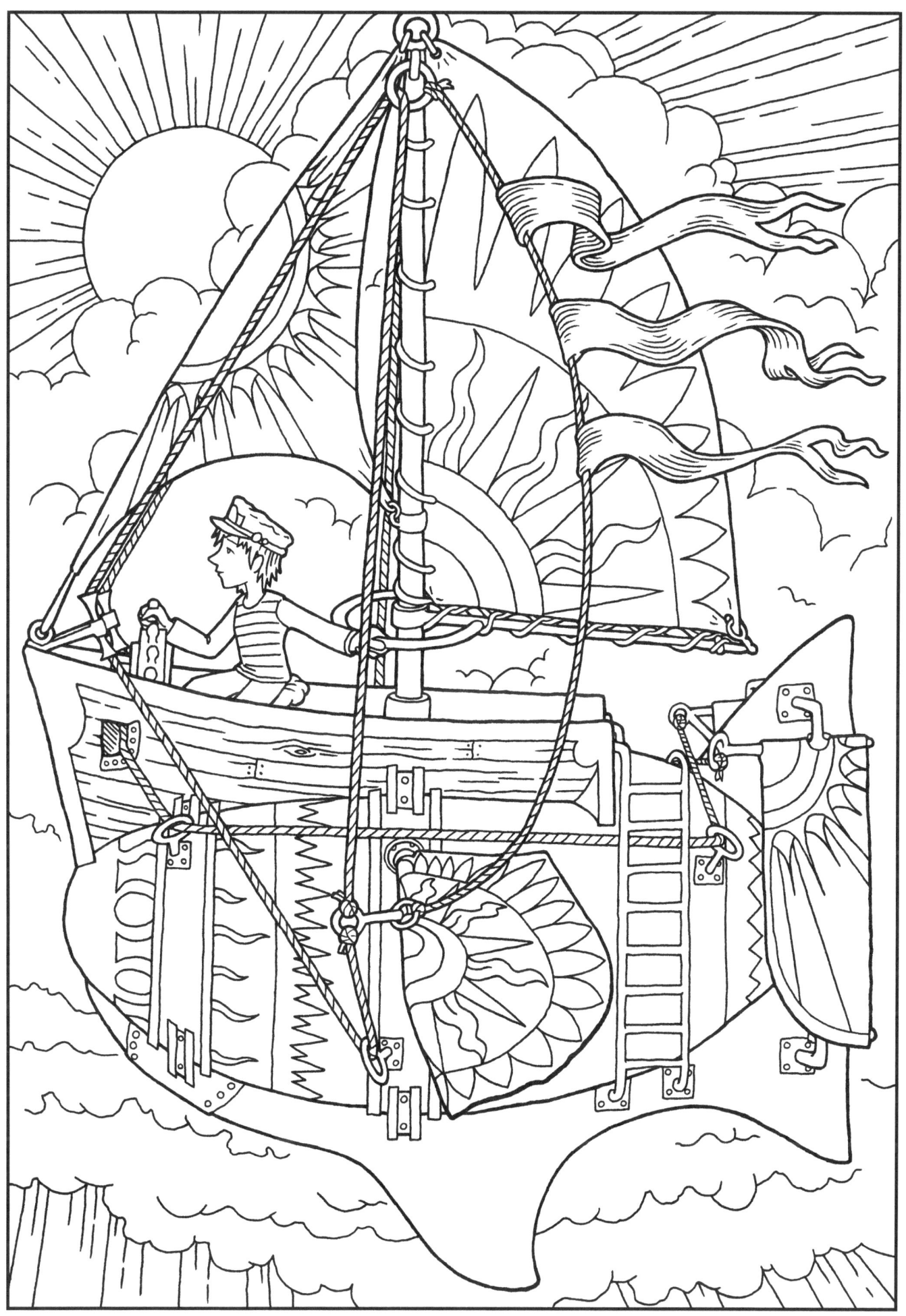

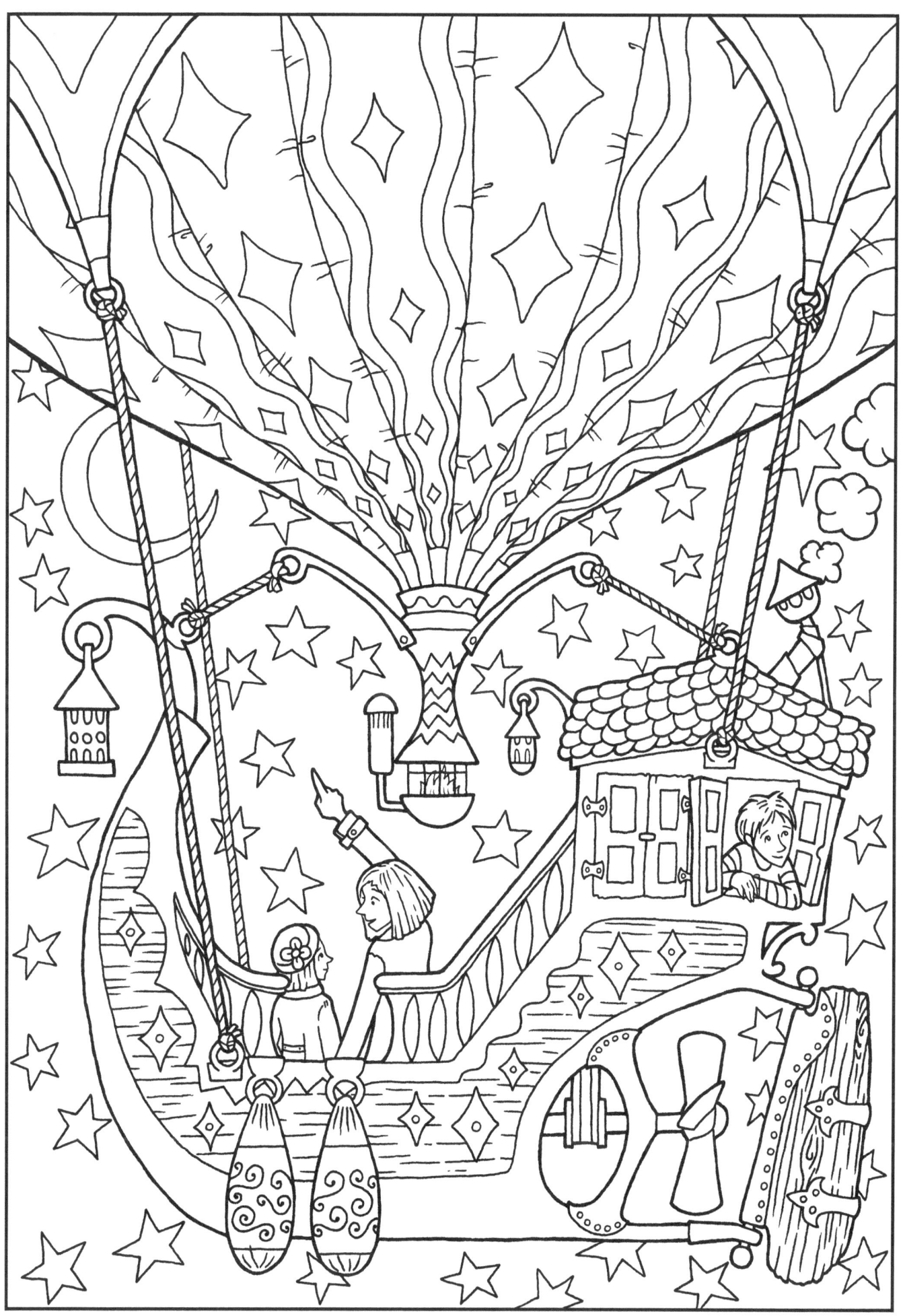

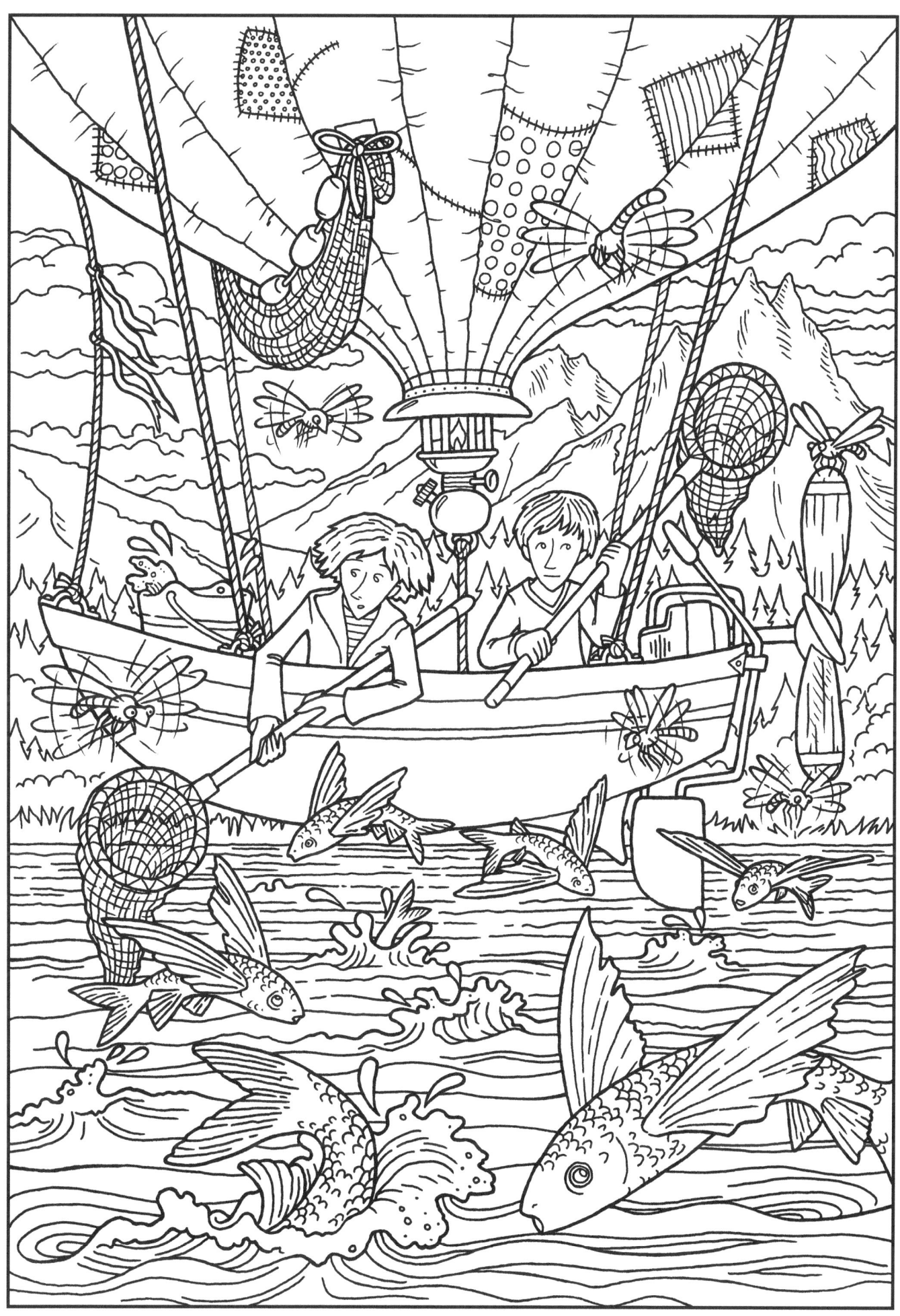

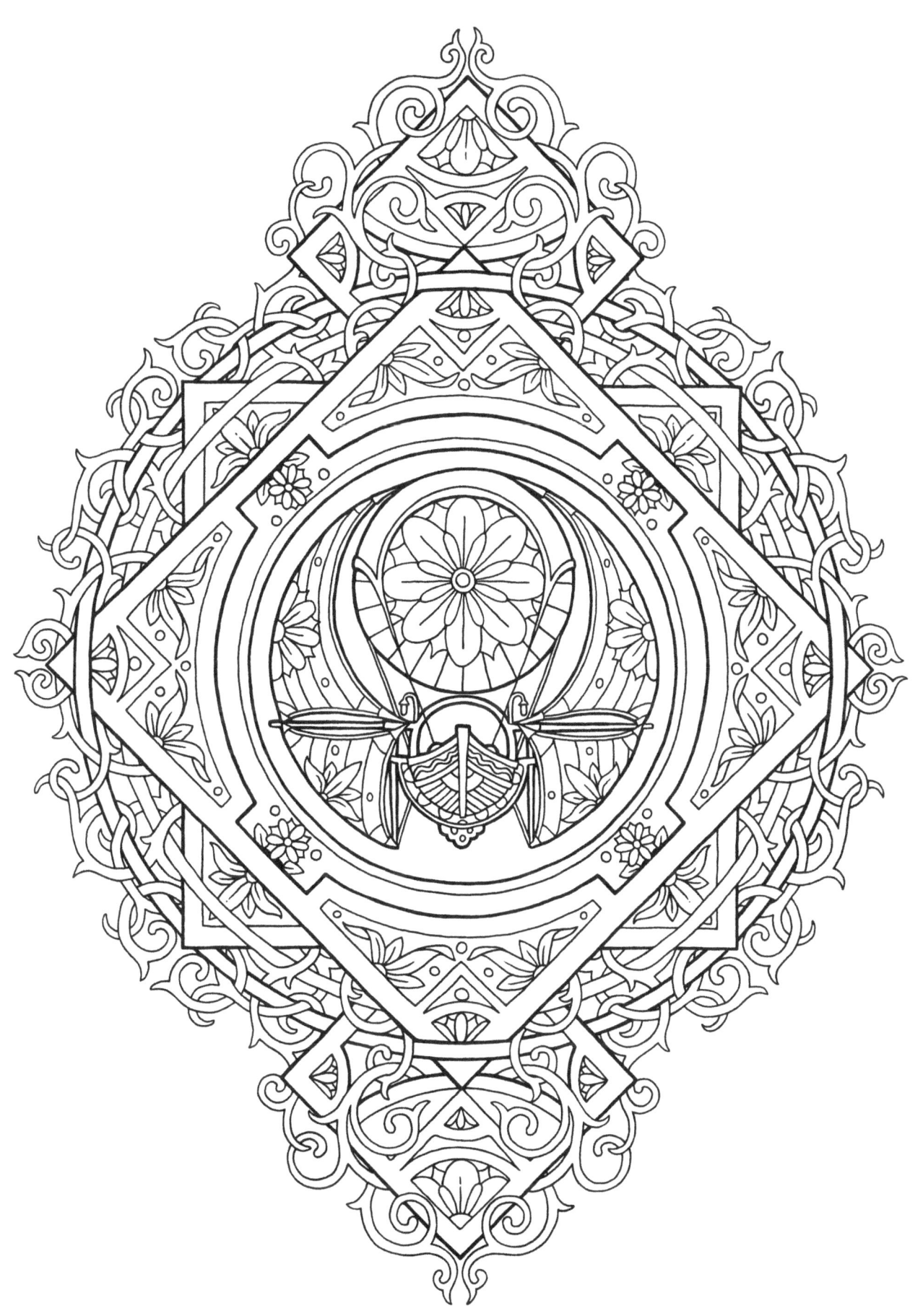

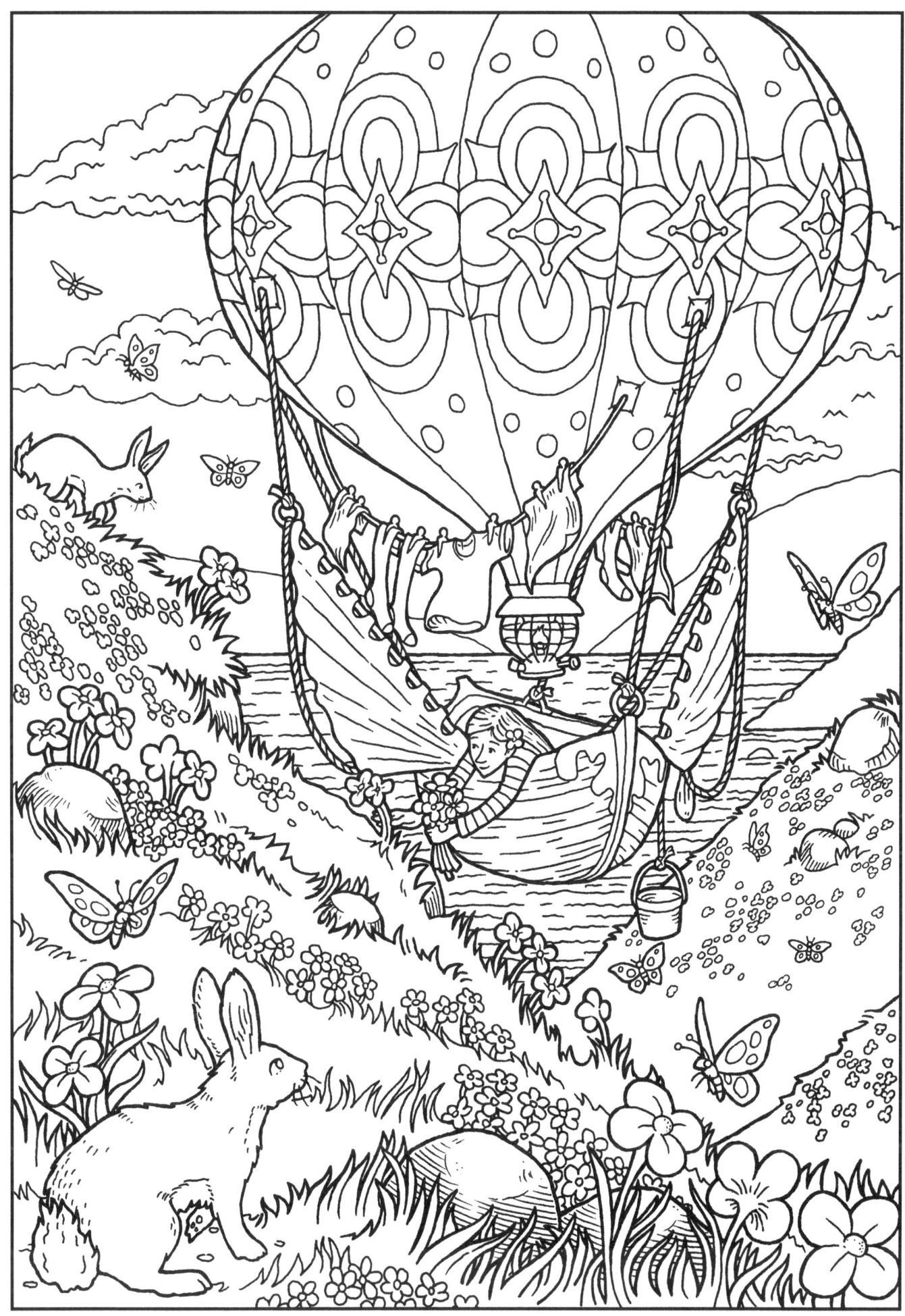

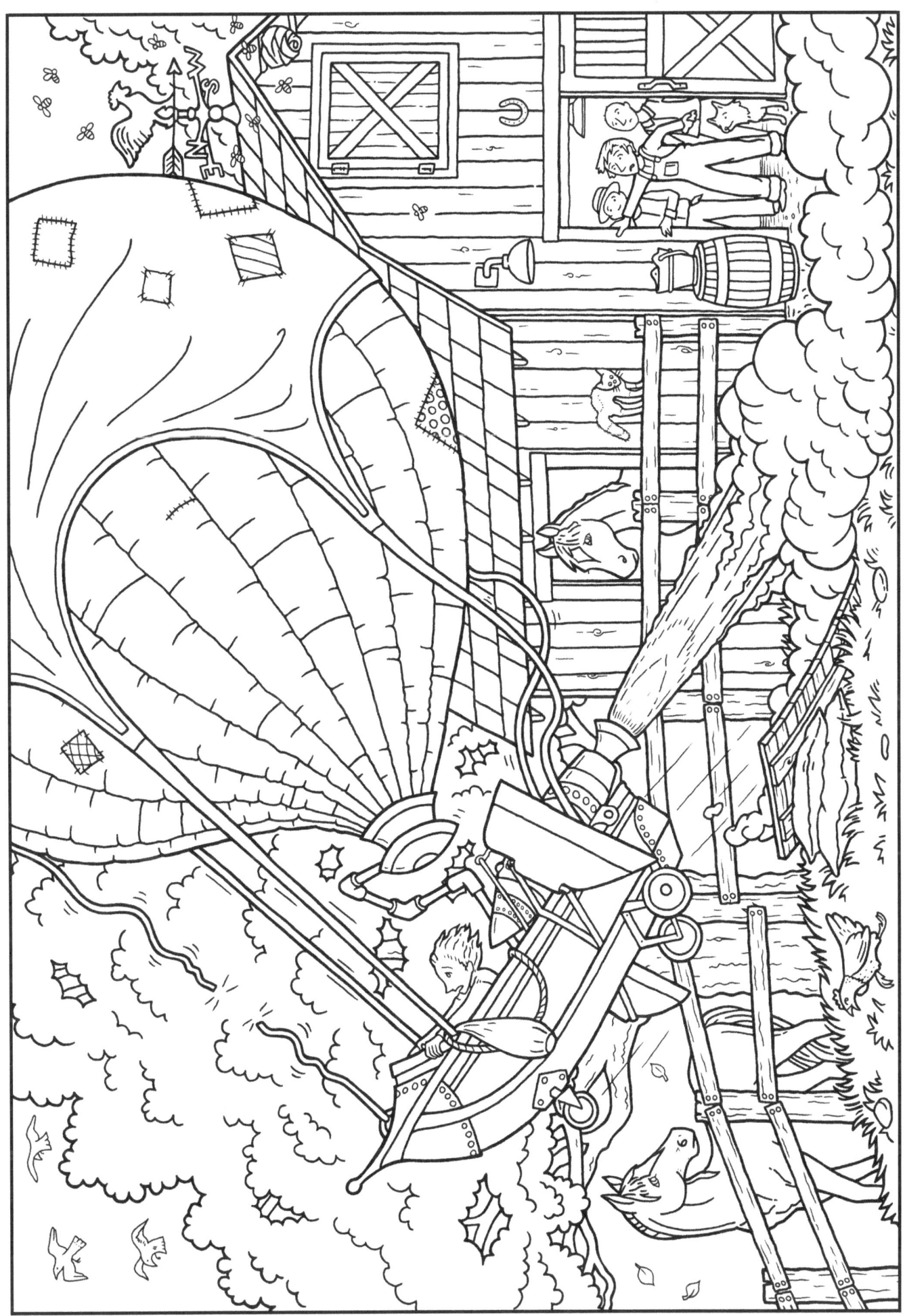

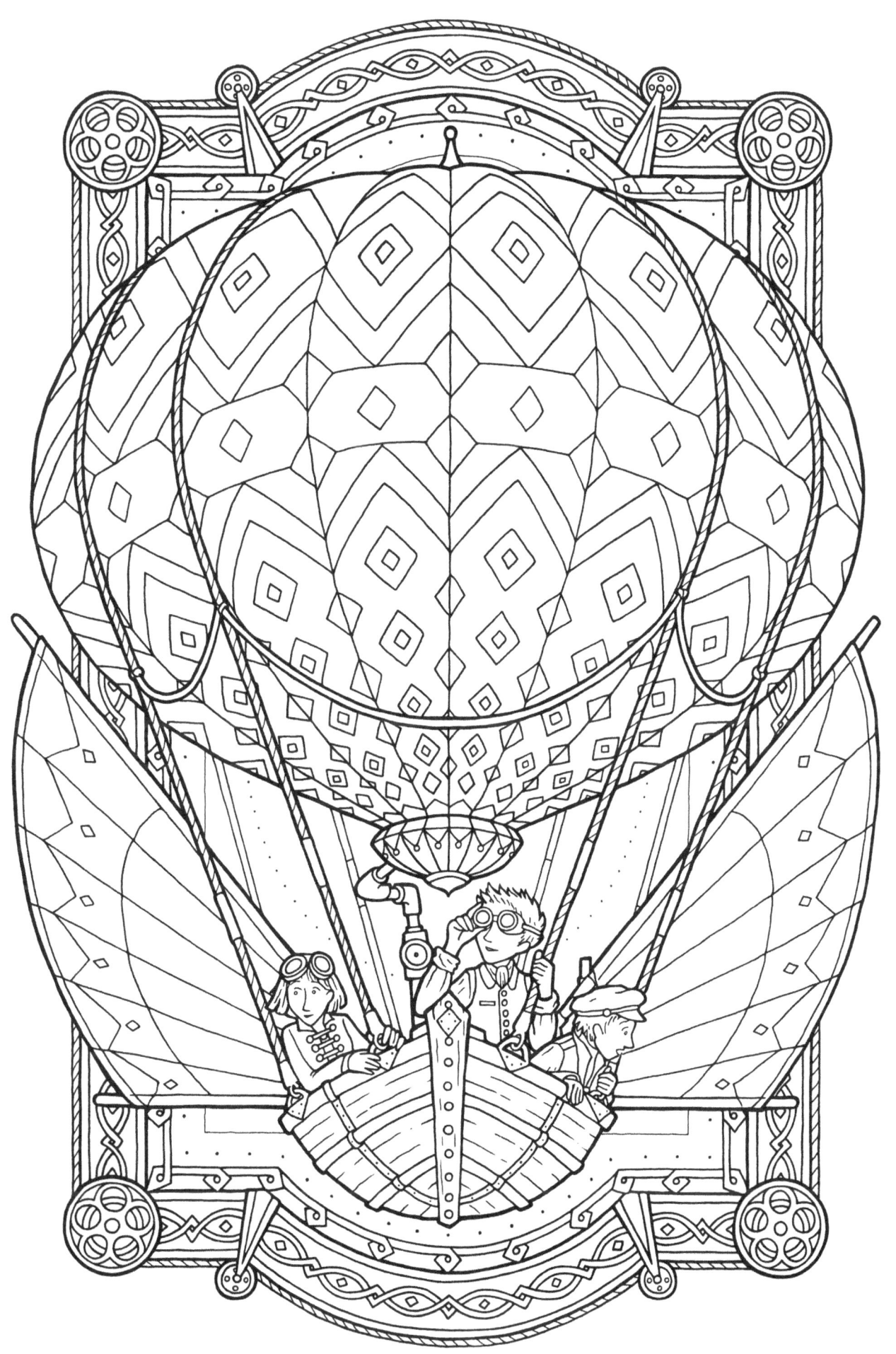

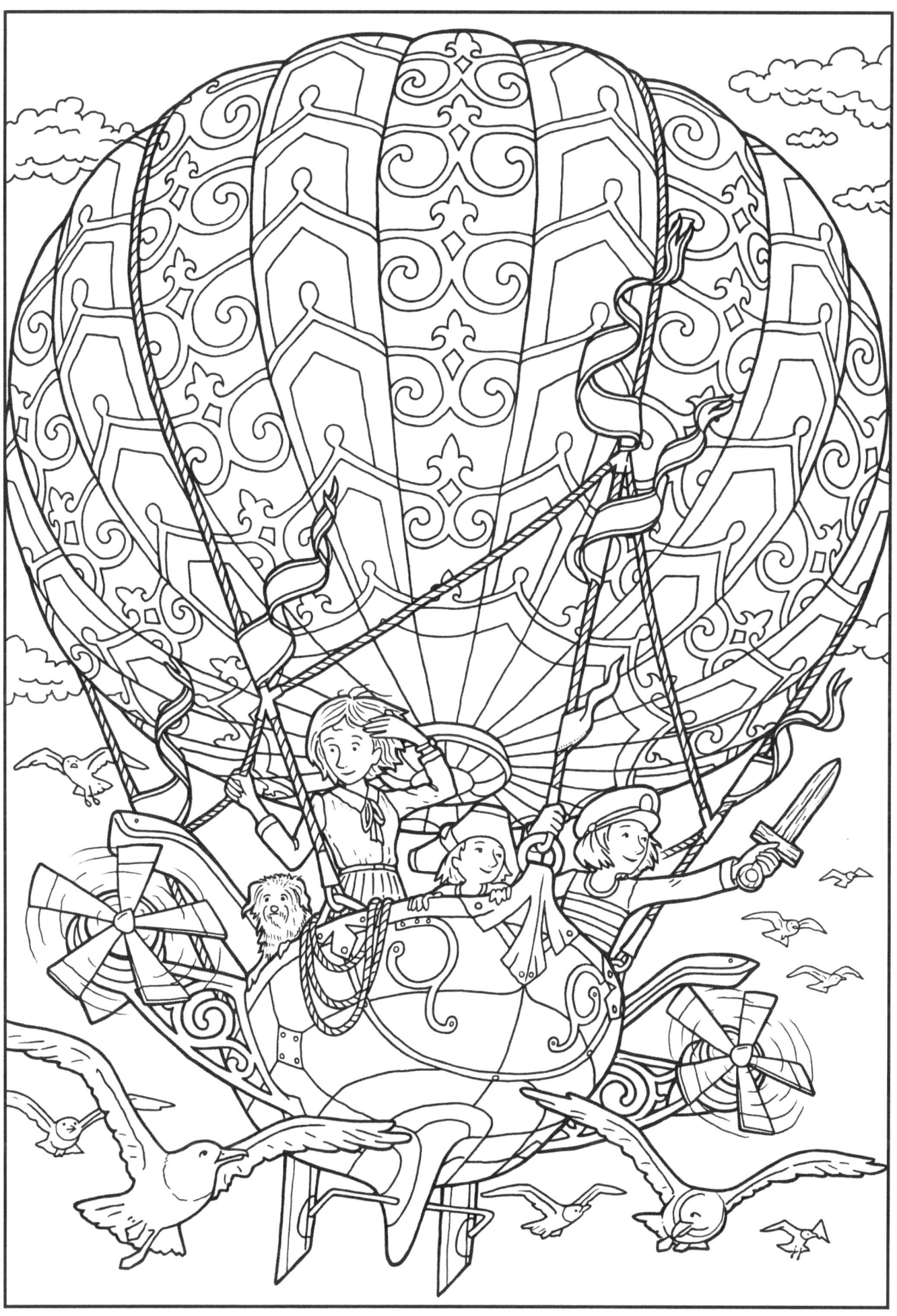

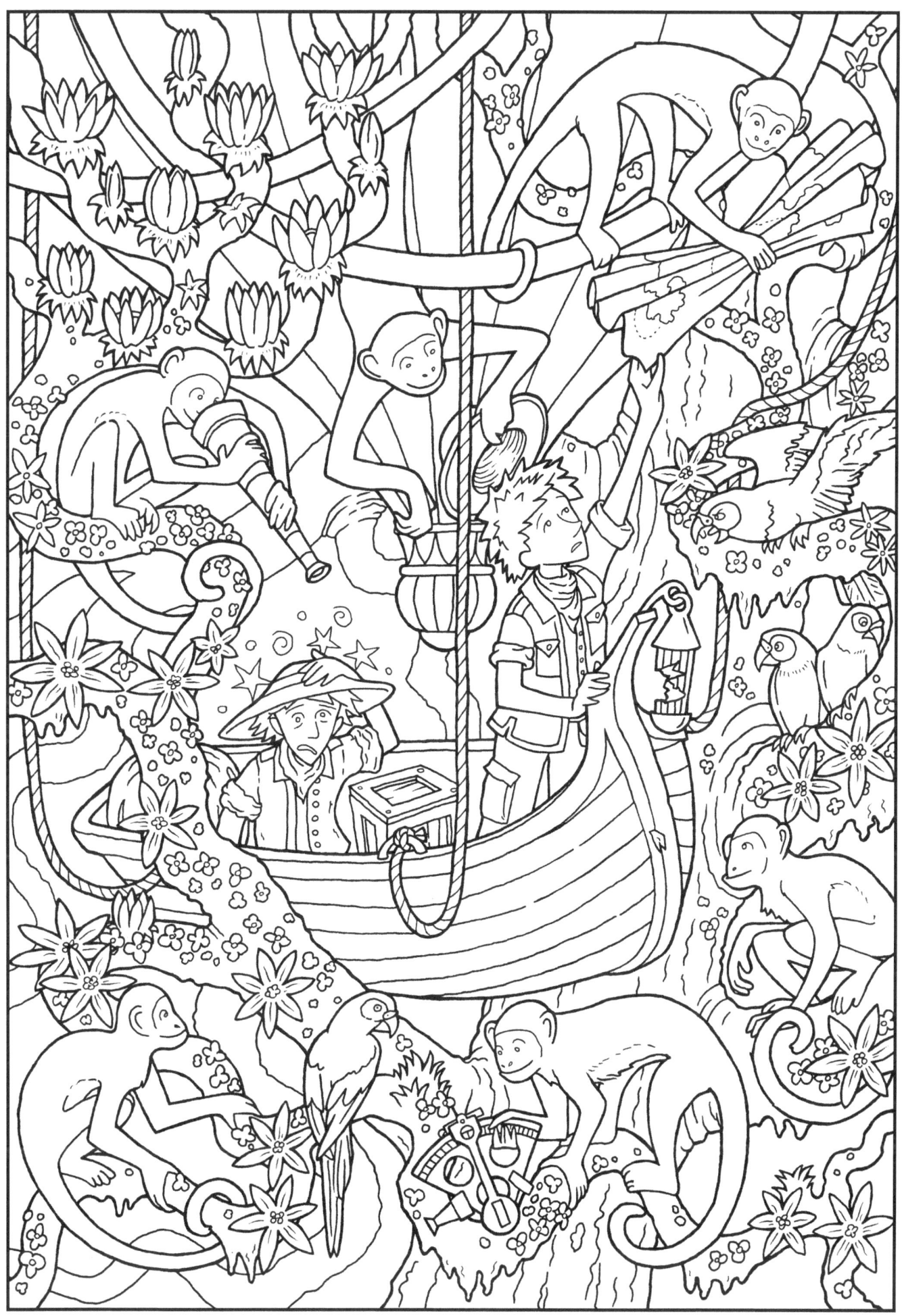

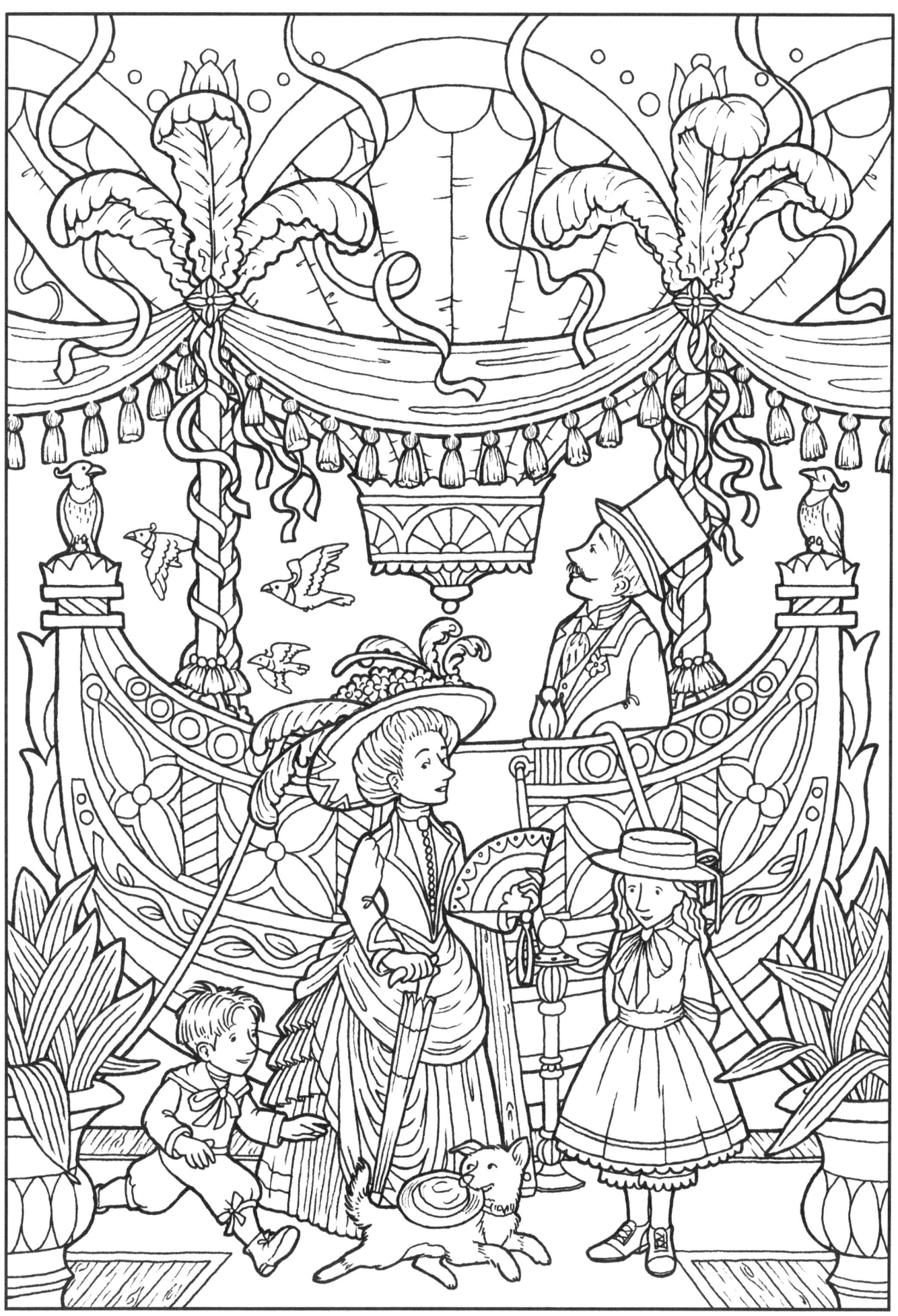

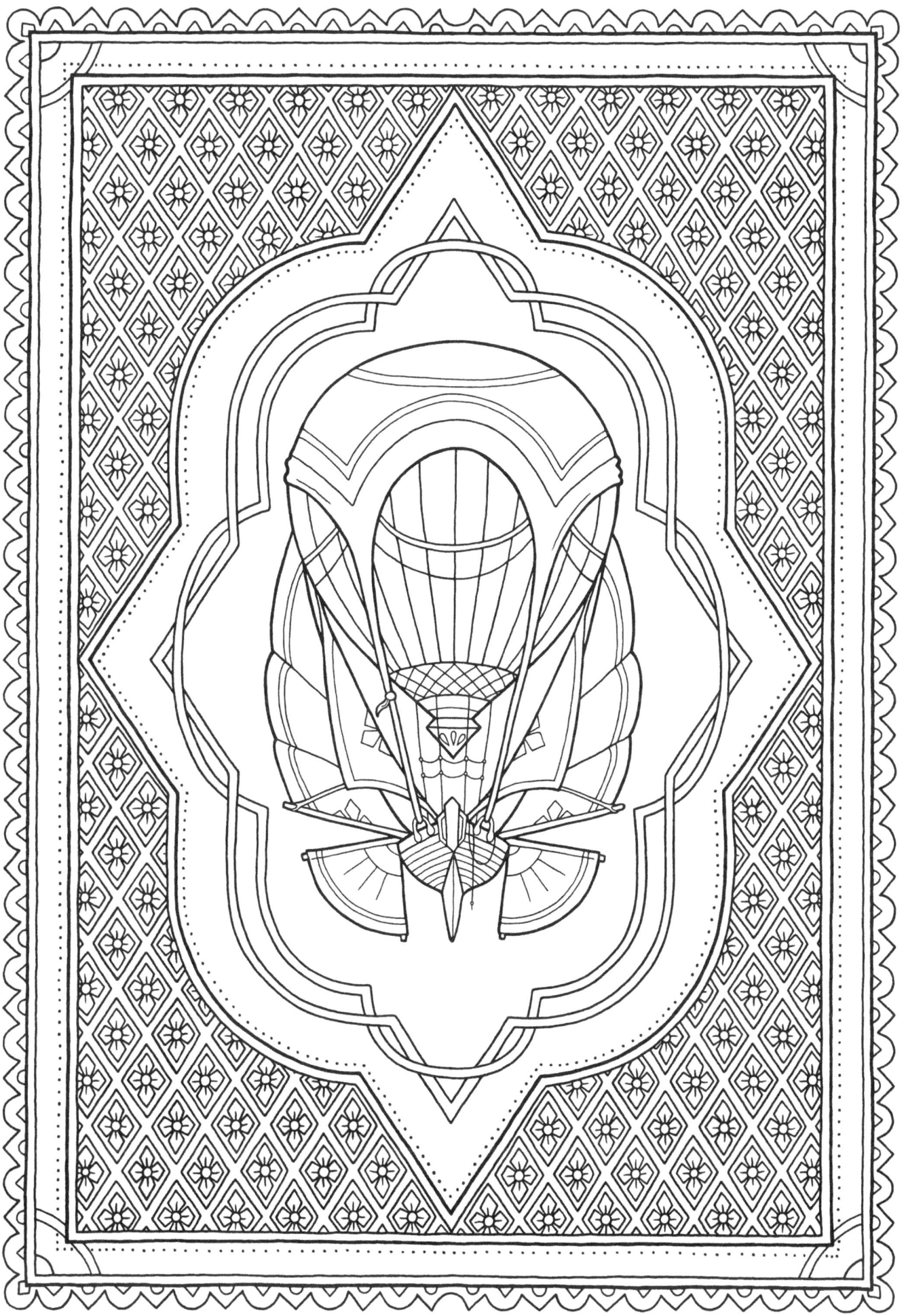

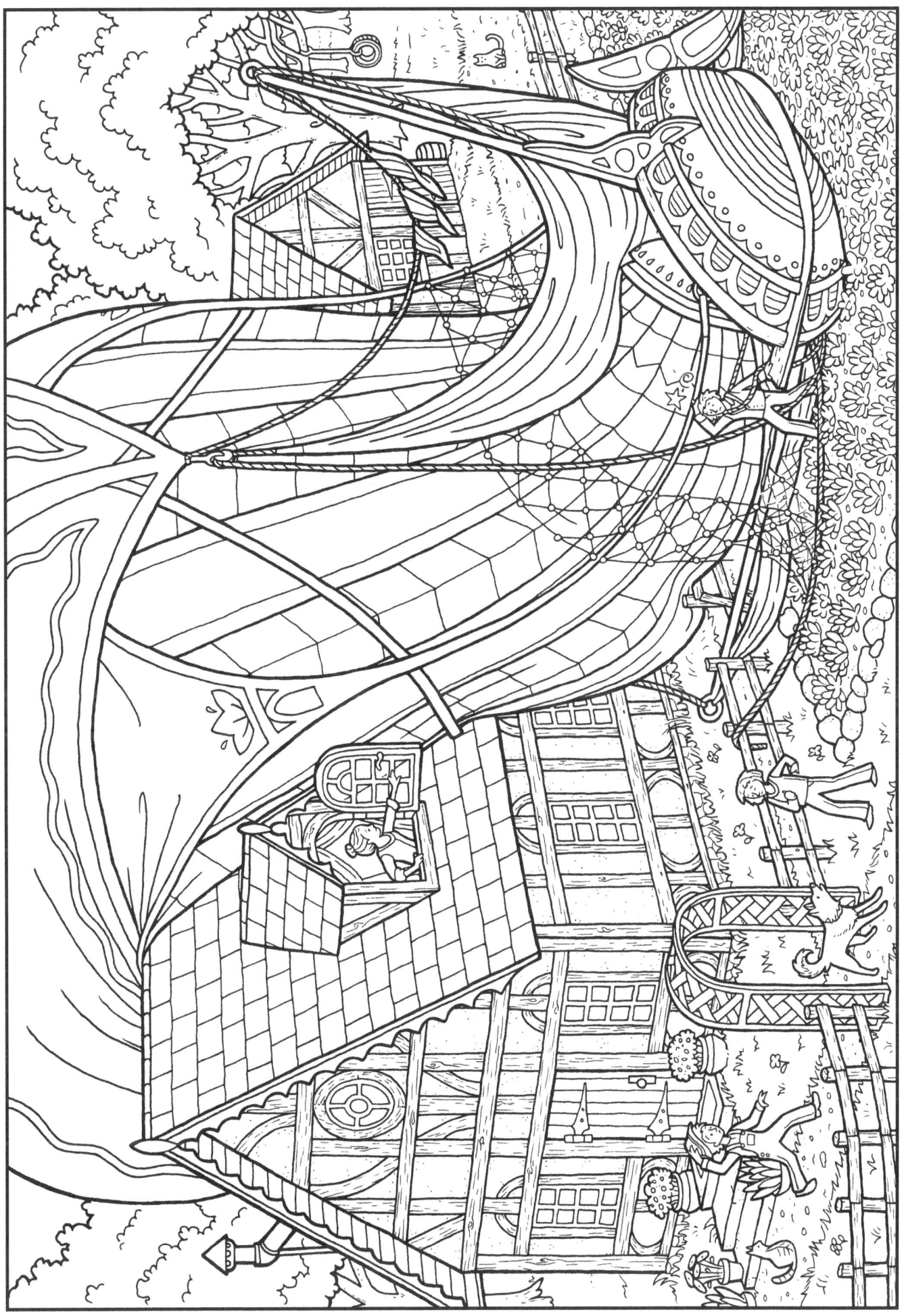

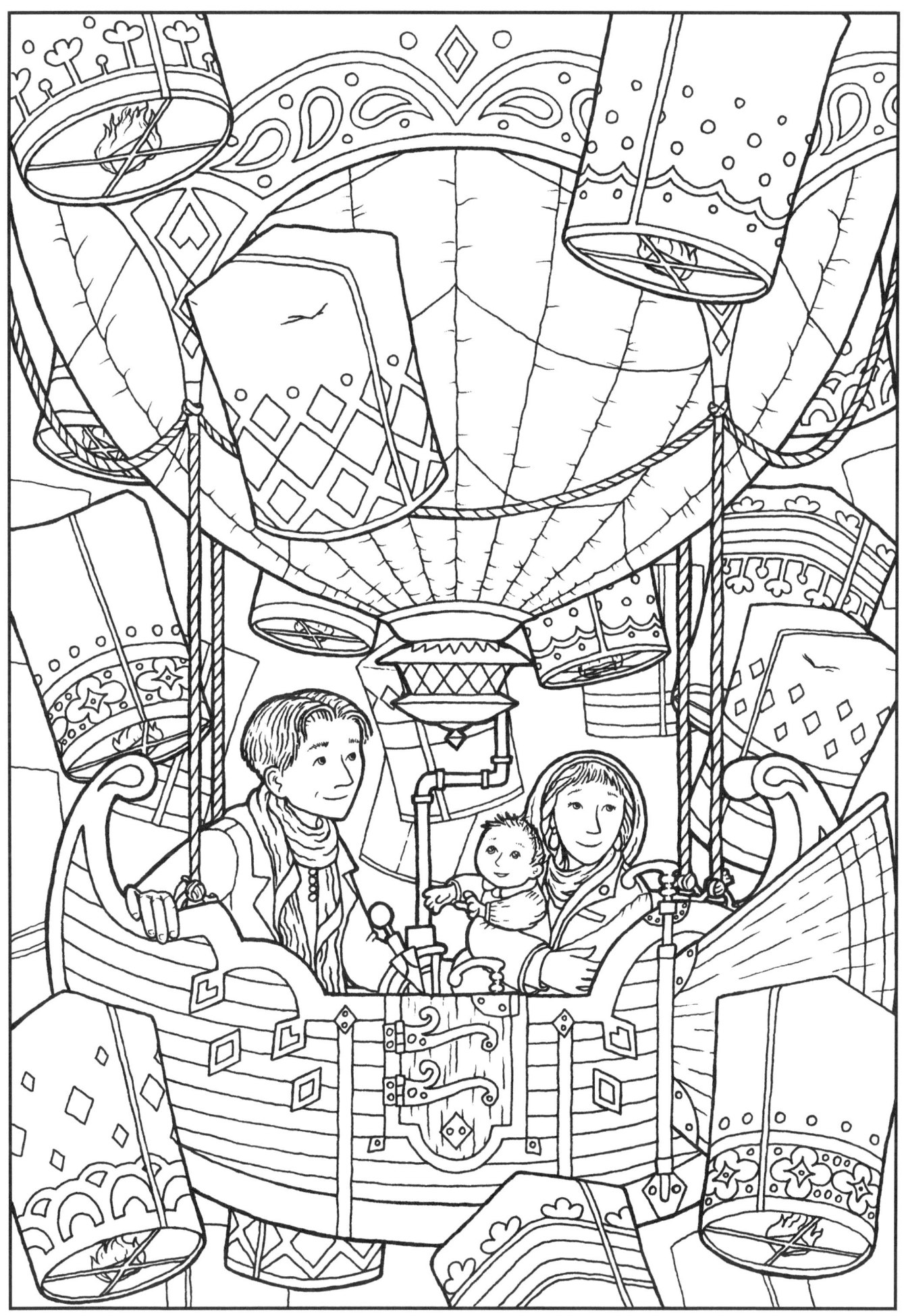

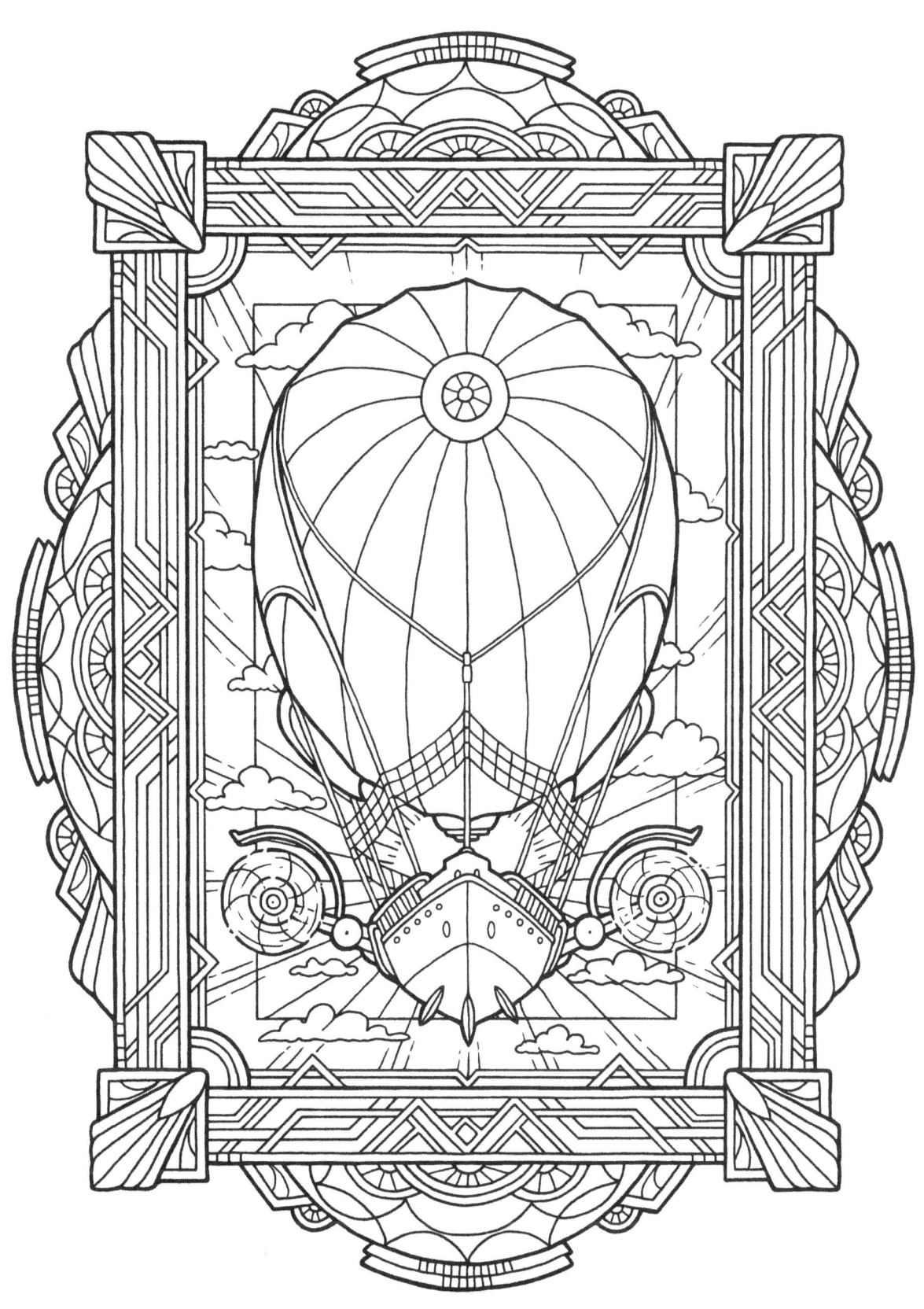

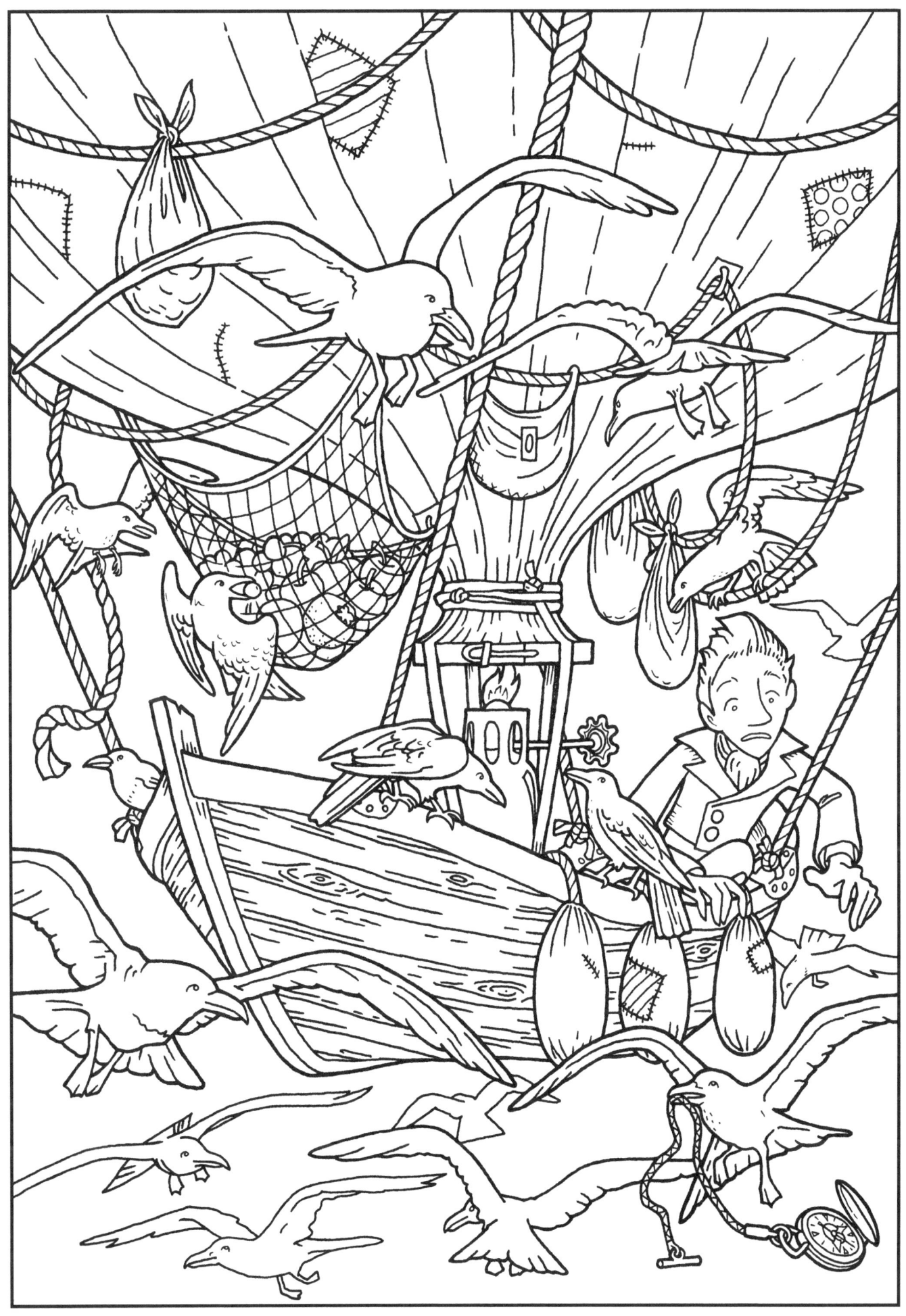

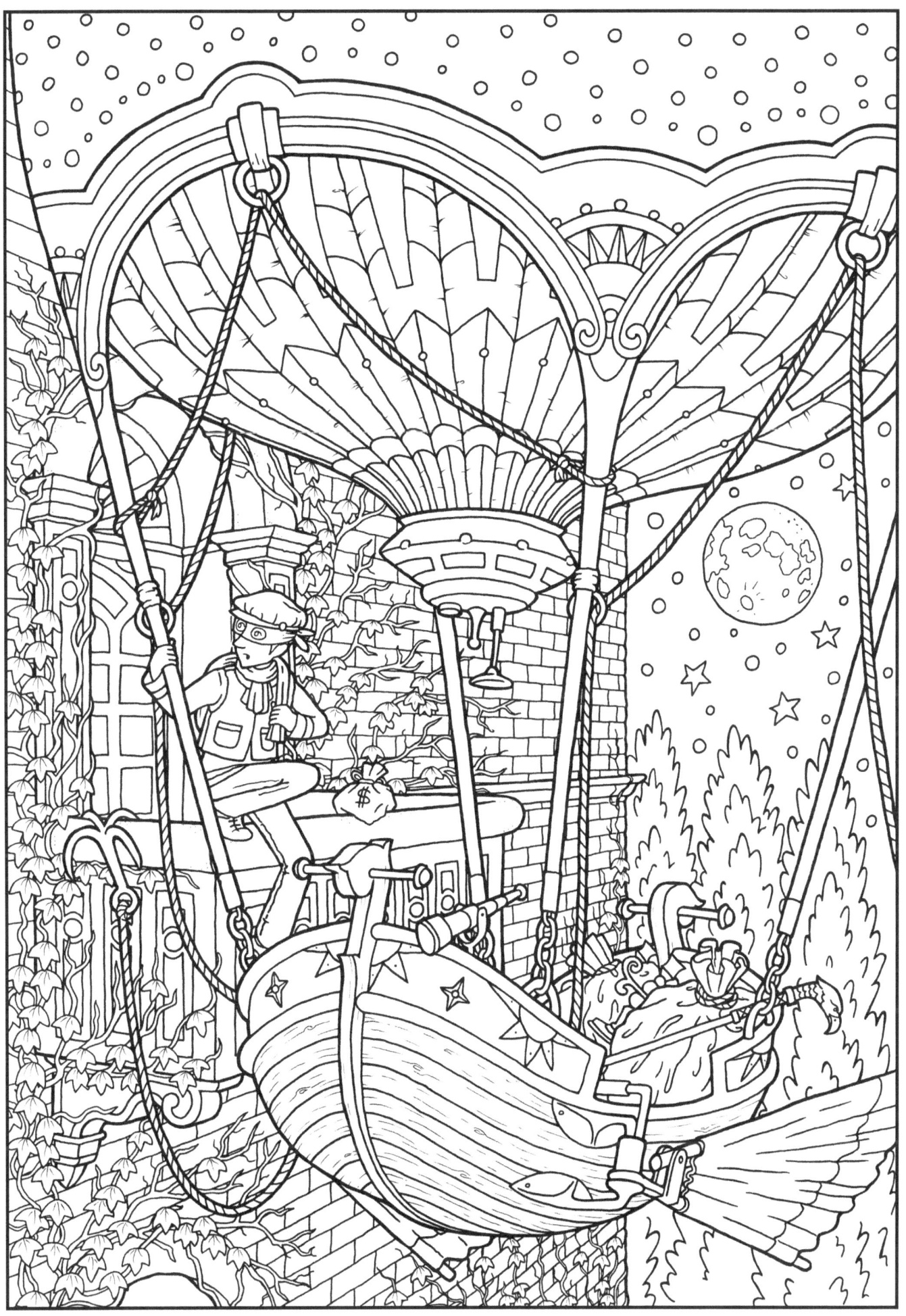

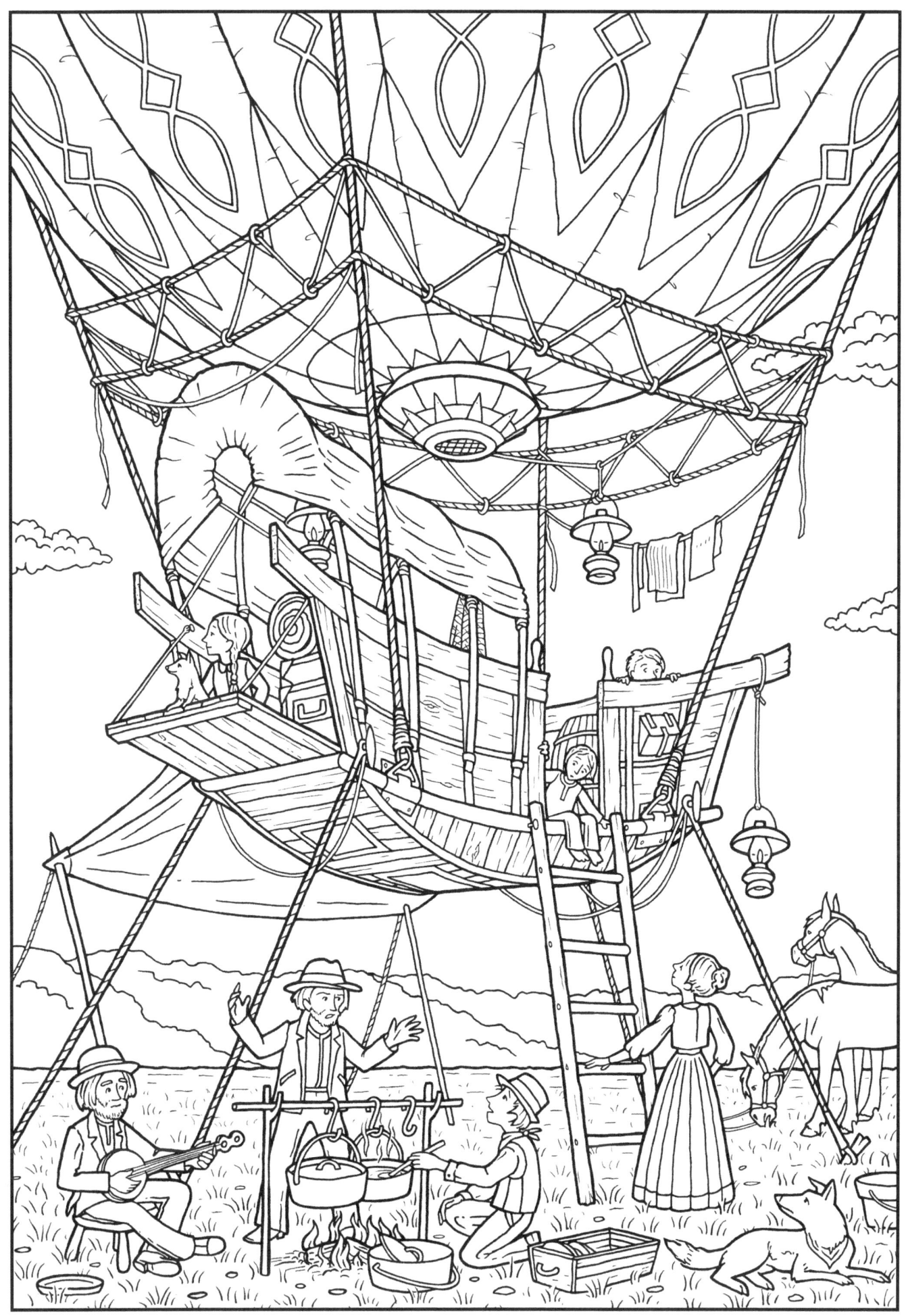

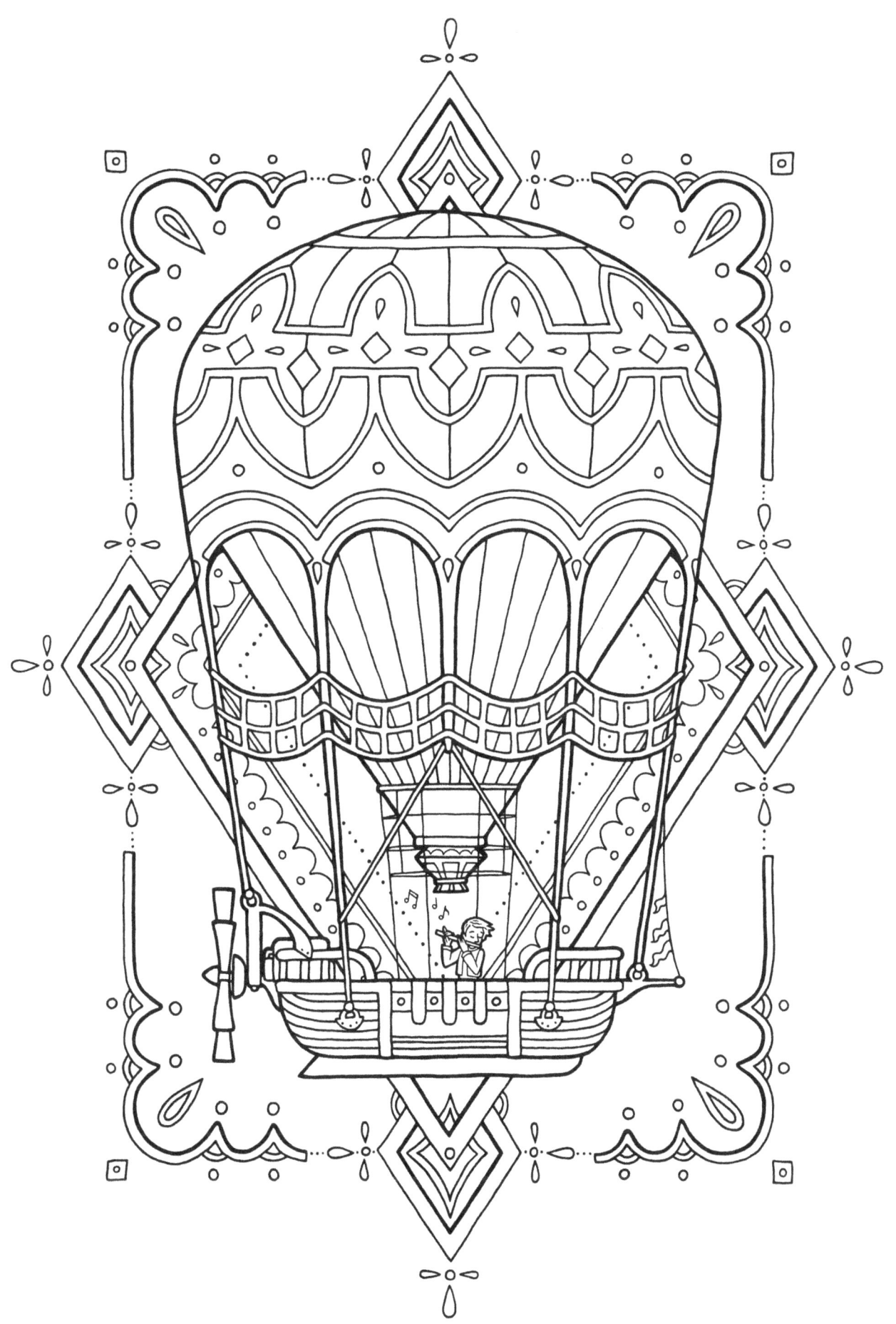

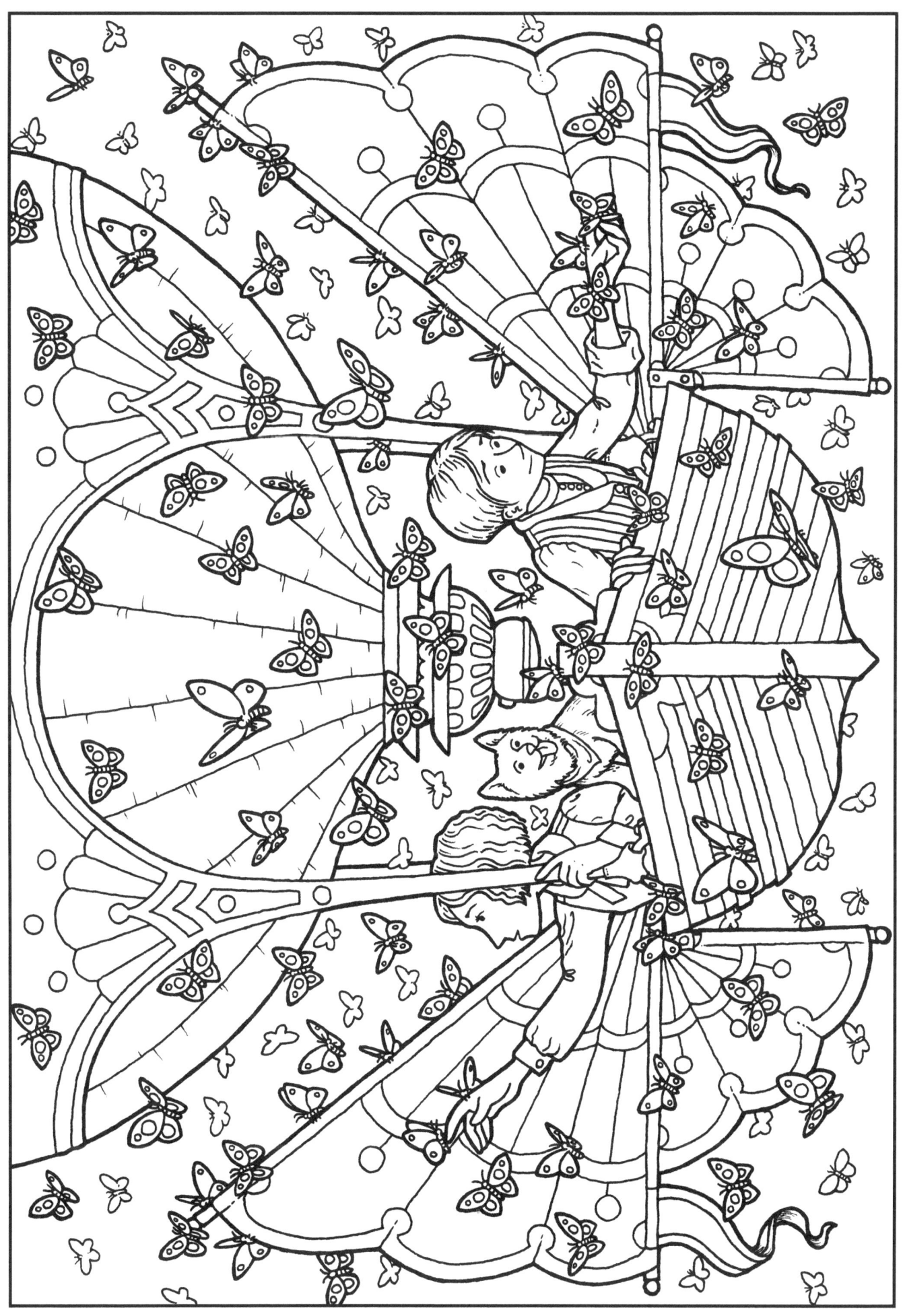

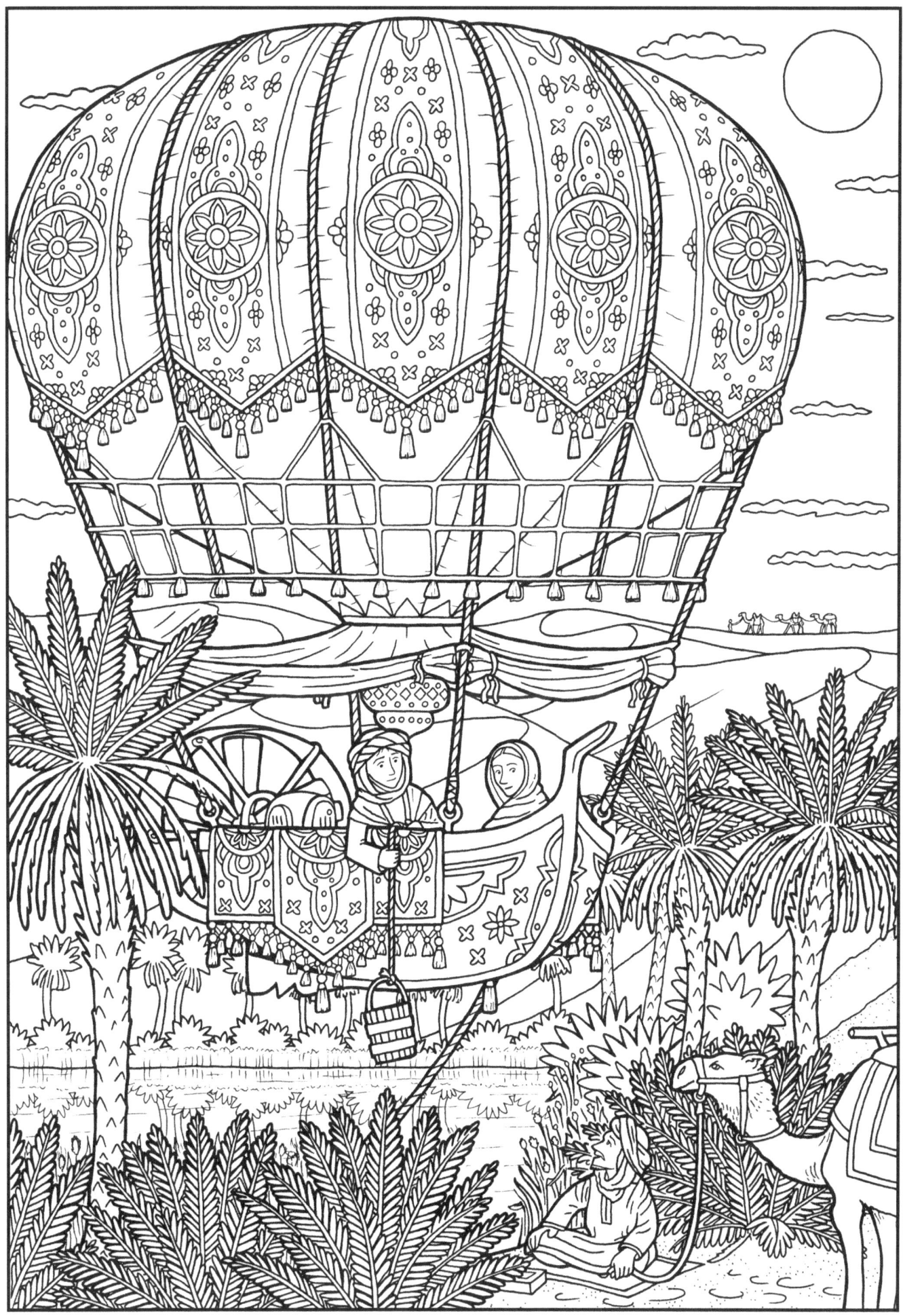

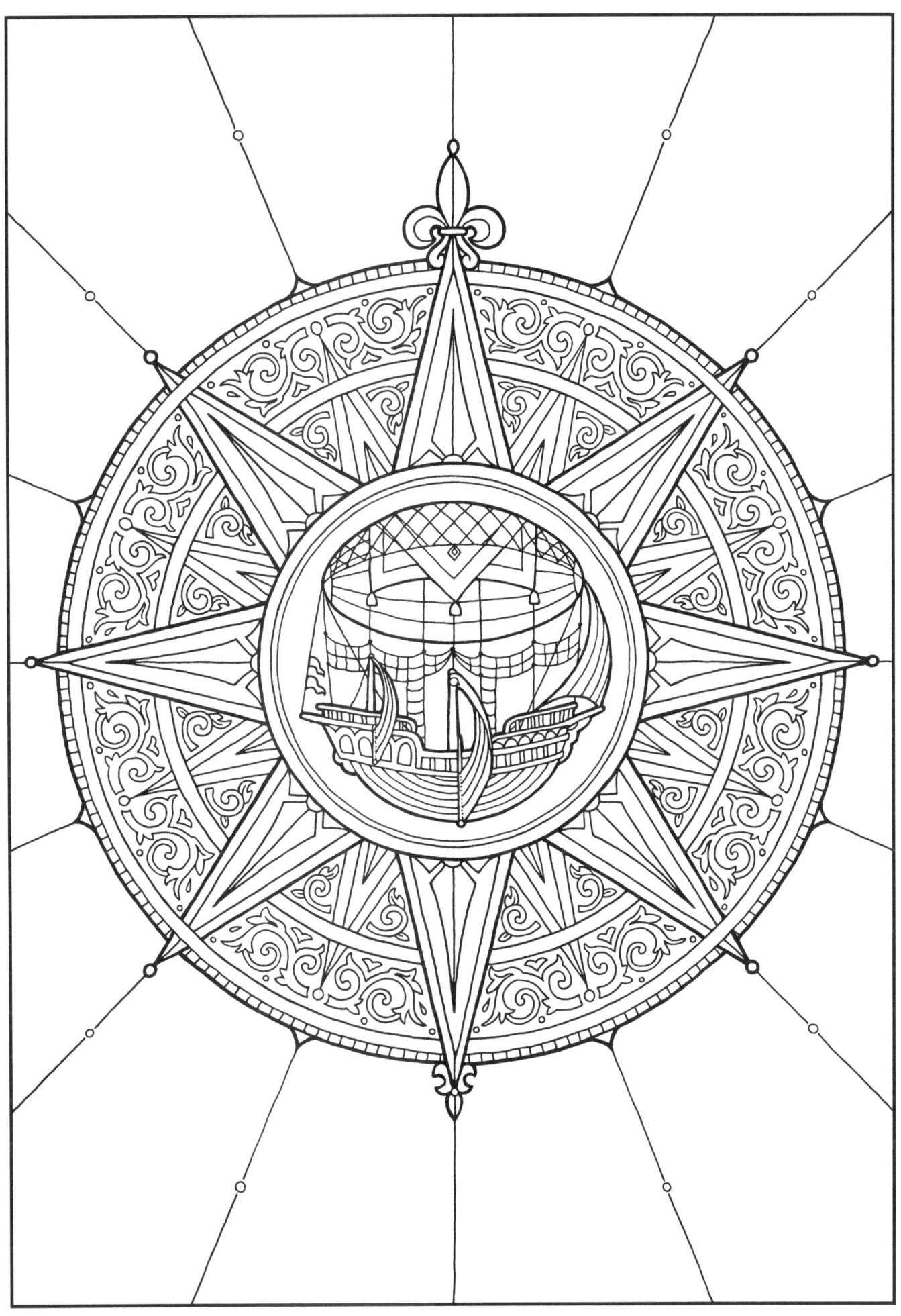

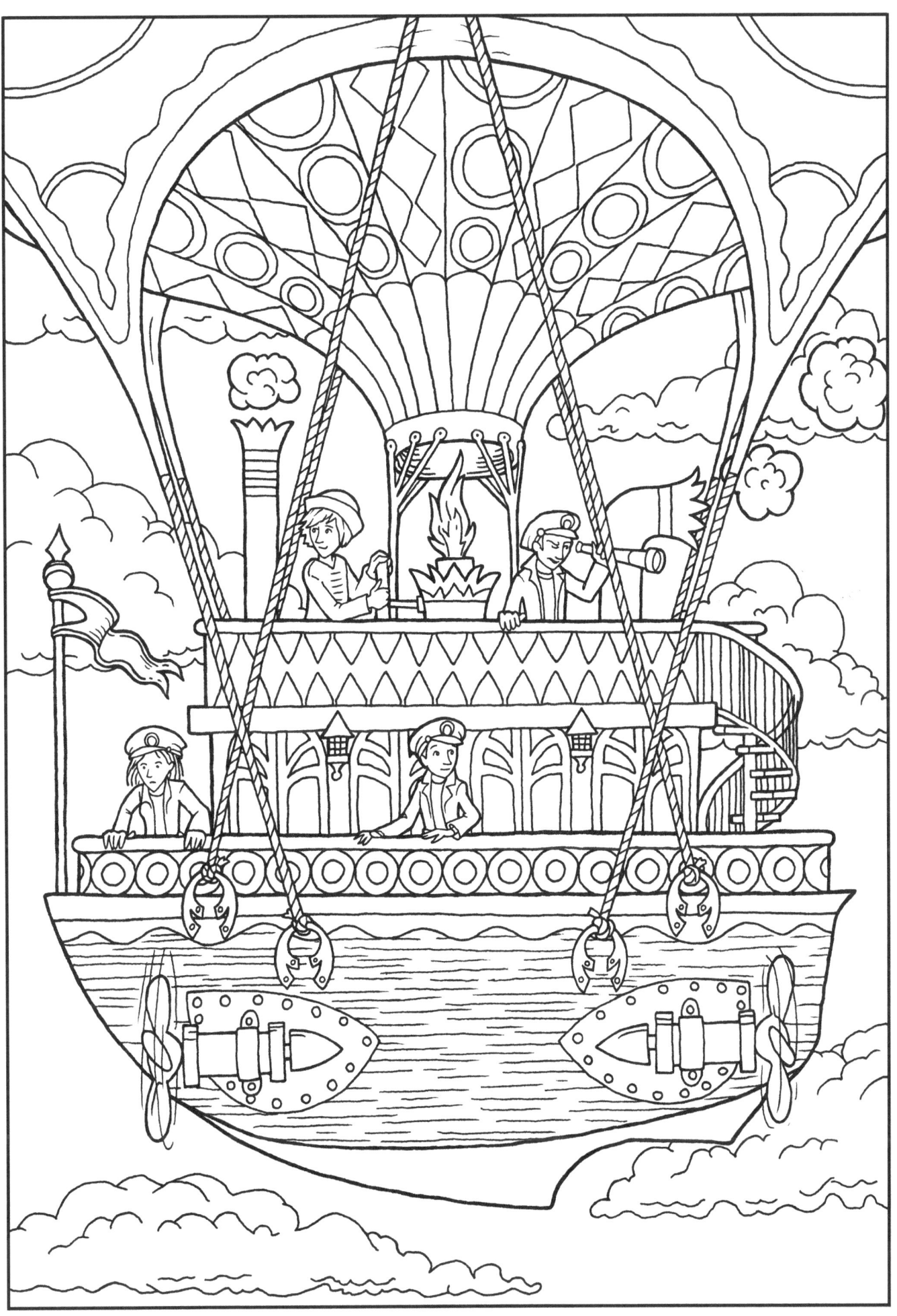

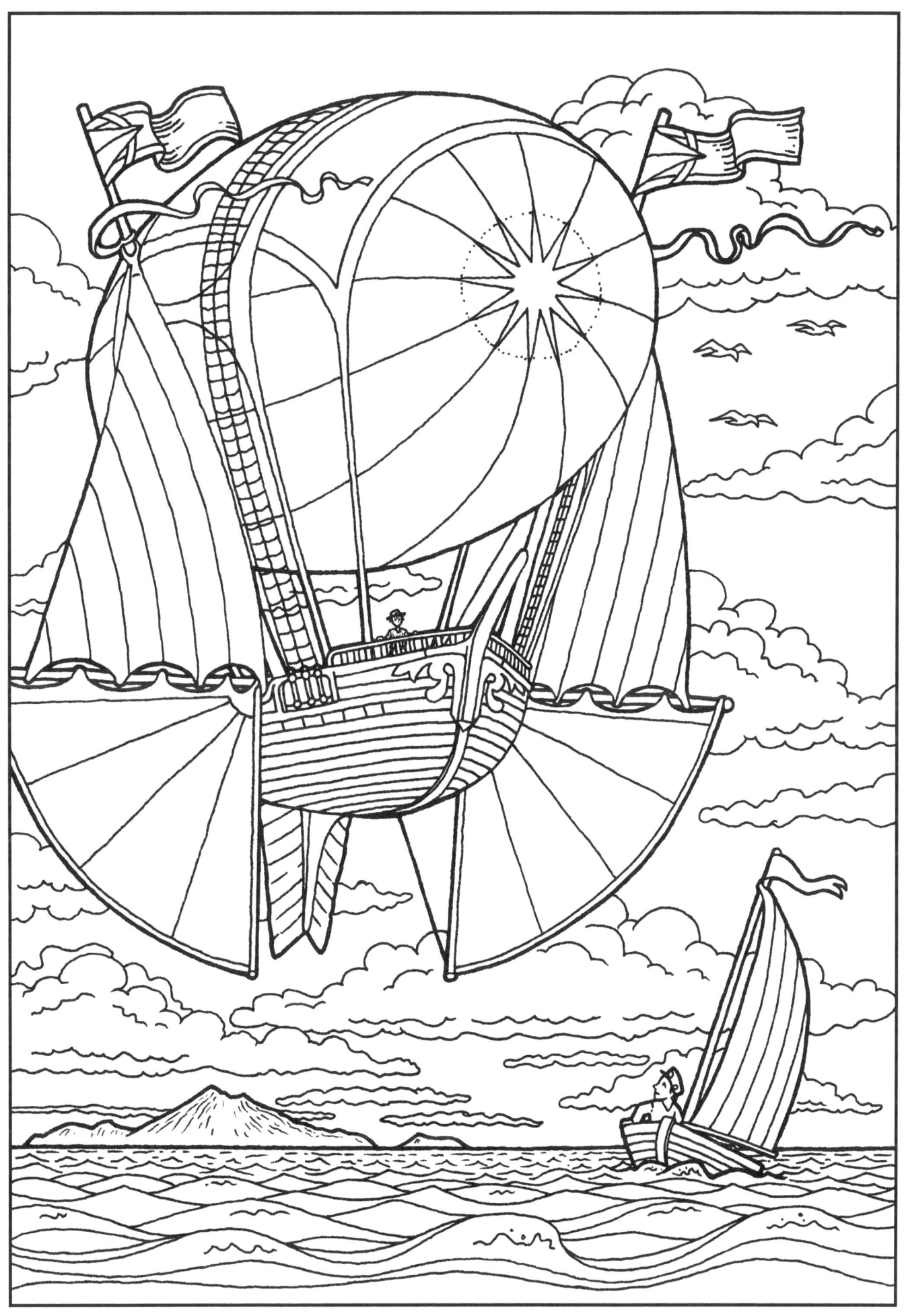

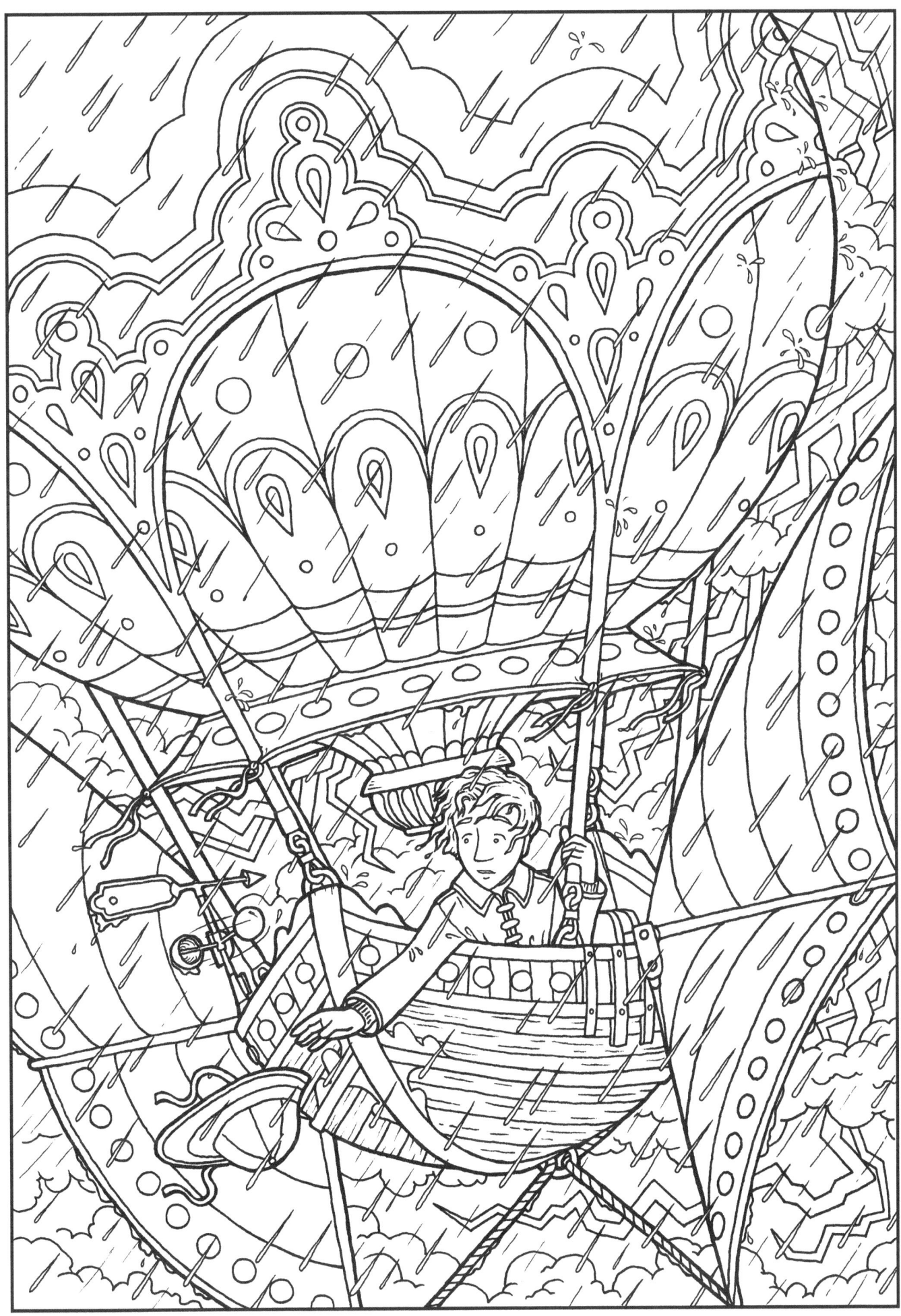

www.ingramcontent.com/pod-product-compliance
Lightning Source LLC
Chambersburg PA
CBHW082255220526
45469CB00009B/3013